MARKLESPARKLE'S CHRONICLES

Marklesparkle's Chronicles

by

Mark Goodwin

CONTENTS

PREFACE

Around the age of just fifteen months, following a long illness, I lost my hearing. My way of looking became somehow enhanced to compensate during six years of silence. Just as the blind are not aware how their hearing is more acute, there was nothing to indicate that my way of watching was any different from others. There was, however, an immediate effect. The absence of sound developed within me a hunger to 'look for other connections' as if to replace my loss with another form of attachment.

As soon as crawling became an option to move around, I would rock the pram onto a side to crawl out and explore. This insatiable curiosity to wander has been a giant in my life. As a teenager, the crawling took me quite far. Before my twenty-first birthday, I had wandered through fifty countries shown green. The Americas are absent since they are beyond a hitchhiker's reach.

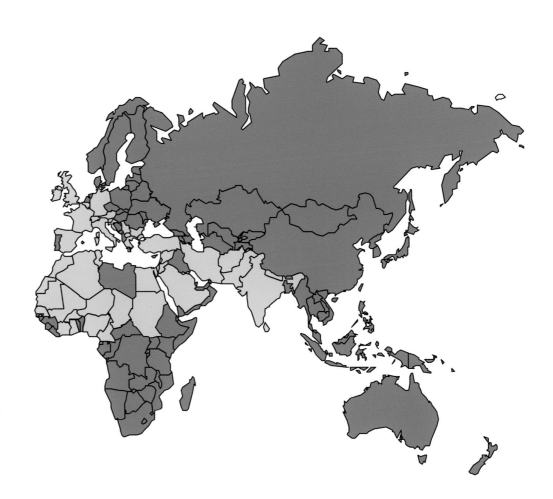

I had a Russian-made-Zenit-E single-lens reflex camera purchased specifically for my first journey to the Indian subcontinent. Before departing, I experimented with 35mm slide film made by Kodak and Fujifilm. One of the attractions of Fujifilm was their processing speed, almost by return of post. By contrast, Kodak often took almost two weeks which tested my patience. This was how Fujifilm became my choice.

Once my travels began, each completed roll of film was posted by airmail to Fuji's laboratory with my Cambridge home as the return address. I did not see the resulting slides until the end of each journey. This was six months later in respect of my time in India and more than two years after my arrival in the South Pacific.

Since my early journeys were to the tropics, I had no chance to make an adjustment for the brightness of tropical light. My reader will notice an over exposure of many pictures in my younger journeys. These have also faded a little during more than 50 years, but they fill me with memories as fresh as yesterday.

There was an unexpected benefit of this film development arrangement. Instead of spending travel money on postcards, my family had regular scenic updates with the arrival of each box of slides. Courtesy of Fujifilm, the 'postcards' arrived very quickly. This was how I communicated with them, and the only way my family could contact me was to write to a Poste Restante where a letter could wait until my journey took me there.

This disjointed communication has an uncanny link with my earliest childhood when my 'hearing' was dependent on choosing to look at my family carefully. When silence enveloped me as an infant, nobody noticed initially. My father however observed a 'quaint habit', whenever sitting on his knee, of my grasping his chin in my small hands and turning his head to face me. This new observation skill was 'hungry' as the sudden silence 'told me' that something was missing. In the absence of sound, we both saw the same pictures. As a teenager, my slides arrived without words. Many of my photographs here are likewise without captions, just as my family received them.

Having wandered through much of Africa and Asia as a teenager, my attention was captivated by the way 'intact' people communicated. Some nomadic tribes adopted me as if they had found their long lost son, opening my eyes to another level of deliciousness and safety. Their warmth led me to explore more; the crawling simply embraced greater distances.

My university education seemed destined for an academic career, but my heart yearned for those times spent with the peoples who 'took me' in a way my own culture had not. Academia was easily and naturally swapped, without a second thought, for beginning my career with indigenous peoples in the Gilbert and Ellice Islands.

The subsequent global spread of my careers has been the flowering of my curiosity.

Two years in the Pacific Ocean included many lands that are too small to feature on the previous map, but I took the time, on the way there and back, to wander in a few other countries. Most of my thirties were spent assisting the developing world with tropical agriculture and my wanderings increased to a hundred countries, as shown on the right.

The end of the 1980s and early 1990s included many civil wars in Africa and some of the farms we assisted were destroyed.

Most of my thirties were spent assisting the developing world with tropical agriculture and my wandering expanded to a hundred countries, shown in green

I was headhunted to work in global manufacturing. A Japanese mentor taught me new paradigms.

In 1992, I decided to work as a freelance coach. A dozen new countries became my focus while coaching leadership in Central Europe after the fall of the Berlin Wall. Following 9/11, I moved to Prague so that new clients could be reached more easily. For the next ten years, my travel originated from Prague and I built up a substantial treasure chest of Czech air-miles.

In the mid-1990s, I met three indigenous shamans; Malidoma and Subonfu Somé from the Dagara of West Africa, and Martín Prechtel of the Tzutujil Mayan in the highlands of Guatemala. They became close friends and often stayed in my London house. At this time, I was also training as a psychotherapist. New vistas opened across the globe as well as within my own mind. Perhaps they were linked.

I spent the next twenty years coaching leaders in over thirty countries, including several times in each of China and Russia. I was fortunate to have time to visit some of their neighbours. Many of those 'additional' journeys were for research as well as curiosity. Discovering the differences between the culture of my host, and that of adjacent countries, enabled me to see more nuances of global cultural differences. This helped to hone my coaching approach.

Often, fate serves up something unanticipated in order to cause a change of direction. There was a sudden surge in my travelling following an unexpected visit to Antigua which triggered a fresh energy. At the same time, Czech Airlines changed their rules and applied a two-year expiry date on all air-miles. My 'treasure chest' had to be used within 24 months. Unable to consume all these by myself, my neighbours also enjoyed free trips to Africa, Asia and the Caribbean. Many chronicles were thus spawned by Antiguan energy and Czech air-miles.

This is how, by 2018, I managed to learn of 169 lands shown green on the right. I have not been motivated to visit all 195 countries of the world as I am still drawn to corners I know well, and where I feel at home. The moment is not yet ripe for a first adventure in Venezuela, Libya, Yemen, Iraq or North Korea. If the right opportunity arises, I would enjoy a wander in a few other unvisited countries, particularly Malawi, and some nations in Equatorial or West Africa.

There have been several 'camera lives'. In 1977, after my return from the Pacific, I upgraded my Zenit-E to a Minolta with a greater variety of lenses. The photographs pleased me much more. But, eventually, I found all the lenses and paraphernalia were too heavy. In 1996, I finally settled on a Sony Cyber Shot instamatic camera. This fitted into my pocket and was more instantly available than a camera where I had to select lenses and apertures. I preferred the spontaneity this camera offered to the extra quality of a fancier camera. Setting up for greater quality often allows the picture to escape. In conclusion, the real benefit of digital cameras is the delete button. This beats my initial budget of one photograph per day on early journeys hands down, and was the real reason for the improvements in later years. The iPhone has also helped with quite a few pictures. I often felt that my childhood deafness had honed my way of looking, and this helps me 'see' the upcoming picture.

By 2018, I had wandered through the 169 lands shown green above.
I have not been motivated to visit all the countries of the world as I am still drawn to corners I know well, and where I feel at home.

This collection of chronicles begins with four very different stories from lands that are reachable in precisely two and a half giant longitudinal leaps, starting in the centre of the Pacific Ocean, exactly 180° away from the Greenwich Meridian, and continuing eastwards. These two and a half leaps cover over two thirds of the globe's circumference. I hope they give my reader a sense of the spread of my wanderings, and their variety, geographically, philosophically and in the different ages of my globetrotting life.

Rather than beginning with my earliest travels, I have chosen to group the teenage chronicles next. The longer story of my most arduous trek across Africa, aged 19, is separately published as Khartoum to El Aaiun and therefore not included here. My first book, Mannership, includes a brief account of my teenage journeys. But, they are presented here with additional adventures and more of my photographs.

Since the 'stans' are all connected in the underbelly of Russia, I felt that their stories should be next to each other, even though different in both time and scope. After the 'stans', I jump back to 1977 in Burma, while on my way home from the Gilbert and Ellice

Islands. Four years later, I returned to Sri Lanka for the Kandy Perahera in 1981.

In general, I have grouped stories together with an obvious similarity, particularly their geography, like the three Caucasus Republics even though visited at different times.

The order of my chronicles here is not chronological. The most recent journeys, Lifou and Tanna, took place in 2018 before travelling was curtailed by Covid-19. I have included them next to another beautiful island, Dominica, which shares some of the indigenous energies.

There are so many other countries I would like to have included, but there is a limit to the size of this book. I hope that my reader can digest my jumping about like a giant bird and enjoy some of the lessons which global diversity taught me.

As a small child, with a strong spirit, my sisters called me 'Marklesparkle'. Soon, the combination of photographs with my infrequent letters became known as 'Marklesparkle's chronicles'.

I should mention that Martín Prechtel taught me to avoid using 'it' since this dreaded word is uncannily often shorthand

for something Holy. I have not changed my teenage chronicles where 'it' abounds plentifully, but since meeting Martín the chronicles naturally acquired either 'his' or 'hers' in the same way that many of the World's languages do. Re-reading the early accounts reminds me how much Martín taught me, as the change of my writing style over the years is very marked. Since we do not always practise gendered pronouns in English, I hope my instinctive choices cause no offence. This is as natural as Mother Nature being feminine, while the sun is male and the moon female. James Hillman taught me that the soul is feminine and flows like water whereas the spirit is masculine and rises like fire. All of us have both masculine and feminine tendencies.

There are many people to thank, and I can only mention a few here. I have been fortunate to meet so many extraordinary guides in different lands; they have known both the way and the stories. Most are introduced by name as they appear. Shamans and tribal elders have guided me to inner countries which enable a greater appreciation of life, especially Malidoma Somé and Martín Prechtel. My life has been made navigable by some extraordinary mentors. Particularly Reuben Uatioa in Kiribati, Lord George Jellicoe in Booker Tate and Professor Hajime Yamashina for Japanese methodologies. My life was helped by several wonderful therapists, especially Robin Skynner, Lionel Kreeger, Claude Pigott and John Schlapobersky. Robert Bly and James Hillman of the American Men's Movement were great teachers. Meredith Belbin inspired me to begin my writing during lovely discussions in his warm conservatory. Michael Oke of 'Bound Biographies' has supported me for several years while patiently editing all of my books. Tony Gray, from WORDS BY DESIGN, has laid out my scripts and pictures pleasingly.

The smiles of children are the best sustenance for a wanderer. Some of them shine forth in the photographs here. I feel so privileged to have had a silent childhood which helped me read the emotional language we are all born with, and thereby drink directly from the looks of the world's children.

During my teenage travels, my parents feared that I would not return. But somehow they overcame this fear of losing me, and always let me wander wherever I wanted ever since I was very small. They have encouraged me by their fascination with my tales and the special Fuji 'postcards'. My grandmother Eva is the woman who always comes to my mind in far flung churches and temples. She was the one who introduced me to the developing world and opened my mind to explore different cultures.

My three sisters and wonderful daughter Alika made sure that I wrote and finished this first account of Marklesparkle's Chronicles.

MARK GOODWIN, London 2022

PAUL AND THE BABAI BEETLES

In Kiribati, formerly the Gilbert Islands, there is only one vegetable, and she is a large corm called *babai*. Babai is well known to Pacific peoples. She is called *pulaka* in Niue, Tokelau, and Tuvalu; *puraka* in the Cook Islands; *pula'a* in Samoa; *simiden* in Chuuk; *via kan* in Fiji; and *navia* in Vanuatu. But, this knowledge will not make us much wiser apart from noting that she has travelled for many centuries. She has been growing in Papua New Guinea for over ten thousand years and has many names. But that's because ten per cent of the world's languages live on Papua. More commonly, she is known as 'swamp taro'. Her fancy name is Cyrtosperma merkusii. The Pacific myths say she was first born in Indonesia and science has finally caught up in confirming that this is right. The myth turns her nose up as if to fret that nothing is right until science says so. But it has been like that for a long time now.

Babai cannot tolerate salt water, though, so she must have been brought to Kiribati on the early canoe migrations, and very carefully packed in some soil. There is insufficient rain on most Central Pacific atolls to irrigate her, but the ancestors of the I-Kiribati discovered how to overcome this. If one digs down into the limestone of the coral sands, in the centre of an atoll, until about a foot above the seawater level, there is sometimes a freshwater 'pond'. And magically this water is always fresh because salts don't travel in through a limestone filter. Freshwater is lighter than salty water and just floats on the top in the same way that cream sits or floats on milk. By digging a pit for her to just the right depth, our well-travelled babai is very cosily nestled in a deep-sided pool. She looks like she is in a nursery there. Since she doesn't like wind, the depth of her pit serves a double purpose. Her giant leaves have thick veins

which seem to pulse as they move gently in a reduced breeze. Suitable locations for babai pits are treasured and often far from a family's house. The babai nurseries are handed down from generation to generation together with all the knowledge of seeding and husbanding the babai plant.

The particular babai pit we are talking about now is in the village of Banreaba, on the island of Tarawa in the Gilbert and Ellice Islands as she was then known. This family pit belonged to Reuben Uatioa who was no ordinary farmer. Reuben was one of the founders of the Gilbertese National Party in 1965. Once the House of Representatives was formed in 1971, he was elected as the first 'Chief Member'. He was very wise as well as quietly progressive. Reuben had tempered his impatience for rapid political progress so as to ensure the best form of Government post-independence. Clearly a wise man who knows that nature cannot be rushed when we hope for a healthy harvest. Reuben was a lovely man. Gentle, kind and interested in everything, especially the grandchildren of his village.

Reuben was also my mentor and a special guide. At the age of just twenty-one when appointed as the last English District Officer on Tarawa before independence, a great deal of guidance on local matters was necessary. I could not have hoped for a better teacher. Reuben encouraged me carefully towards decisions that were gentle and helpful on Tarawa, helping me to serve as a bridge from the colonial past to a fully Gilbertese future. Knowing myself to be the last in a line which went back to Arthur Grimble, I was anxious not to upset my hosts nor do anything toxic.

Speaking of toxic, the babai plant is very toxic. Babai is a rich source of carbohydrate and calcium. But, if not properly prepared, the sensation can be shocking. The mouth reels as if needles have been inserted right through the cheeks and tongue, or so Reuben told me. Luckily, Pacific Islanders know how to neutralise any toxicity of this giant corm by slow cooking in an earth oven with coconut cream. She is then delicious and tastes more like a nutty sweet potato with an occasional whiff of vanilla bean. I cannot resist adding that, apparently, the swamp taro is the largest plant in the world which produces an edible corm and, in the centre of the Pacific, she is growing on one of the narrowest islands on earth.

I enjoyed my regular visits to Reuben and his family for advice. I sometimes felt like pinching myself with my good fortune to have such a friend and guide who was so wise, an elder among elders with his experience as the first leader of the House of Assembly. The evening of his life coincided with the beginning of my career. We had the same objectives. He enjoyed my practicality. With his support, there was no need for me to doubt my energy or enthusiasm to 'get things done'. The journey up the coral reef mud road to his village was by motorcycle, a mere fifteen minutes from my house overlooking the ocean in Bairiki village. To say 'motorcycle' is a little strong really. This was a 50cc light green Honda ladies' model and rather sedate, but the perfect transport for all eleven miles of Tarawa's main road. With anything faster the island would have been too short. I am not sure why I say 'main road'. Perhaps this is a habit, or simply because there was no other road on Tarawa.

Reuben's babai pit was directly on the narrow path from the 'main road' to his house. I had to pay particular attention to drive carefully around the edge before riding up to his porch. We spoke about many things of great importance to the local elders but not about the babai plant, except in passing. She was there, carefully tended by Reuben's family and carefully navigated by my motorcycle, and so this pit might always have been but for the visit of Paul.

As a child, my mother used to sing in a choir and she had a close friend, Erica, who sang with her. One of Erica's sons was called Paul. We knew each other from the few occasions that our mothers took tea together in the garden and 'dragged their children along'. We were not in the same school so we did not meet often, perhaps once or twice a year. But Paul was my age and a nice boy. Geography can change relationships overnight, though. Paul had finished his degree in agriculture and was travelling

around. He found himself in New Zealand and a letter from his mother suggested that he visit me as I was in the same neck of the woods, or whichever expression Erica had favoured. It is true that the Pacific Ocean is a body of water that New Zealand and the Gilbert Islands share, but we are not exactly in the same neck of the woods. Four thousand kilometres by sea would be a better description. Never mind; when Paul wrote

to me and asked if he could 'pop by', I said, "Of course, I would be delighted, and there is a spare room in my house."

In the coming days, I began to look forward to Paul's visit. The idea of a family friend from Cambridge would be most interesting and pleasant. I wondered how Paul would get to Tarawa, but of course he would figure that out. It was a lovely surprise when he arrived a few weeks later.

And such a pleasure to be able to talk about our Cambridge homes and families over dinner each evening. Paul's stay got longer. This is easy to understand if one knows the Gilbert Islands. They are one of the few paradises left on earth. Or, 'left on water' might be a better description.

After a few weeks, Paul decided to do something useful, but what? Having a degree in agriculture, I suggested he contact the Ministry of Agriculture and ask how he could help. Now, unbeknownst to me, one of the most pressing agricultural issues at the time was the babai beetle. How had I missed this information? A good District Officer should know of the troubles of the local population. They had only the one vegetable, babai, and there was a beetle which could ravage her roots. Clearly this was an urgent matter. The next day, after my motorcycle ride to Reuben's house and refreshed by one of his king coconut juices, I introduced the idea to our former Chief Member. "Wonderful," he said and then quickly added, "and Paul could use my babai pit for his research. Then we can both follow the matter with interest."

Thus was set the next two months' research in Reuben's babai pit. How to conquer the babai beetle? I had never met this beetle, so the mite was a mystery to me. But, during our dinners of fish and rice, and of course babai, Paul introduced me to the specifics. The babai beetle was about nine millimetres long apparently. After further explanation, an image of a vine weevil came to mind. The challenge was how to catch him.

Being fresh from his degree, Paul thought quickly and knew he had not much time. Only about eight weeks of his planned stay in Tarawa remained before returning to Cambridge. Somehow, in just eight weeks, he had to trap the beetle which was causing the babai so much grief. Paul decided that it was too dangerous to use a chemical from the Ministry of Agriculture to try and kill the beetle owing to possible harmful effects on the natural environment. With this, I agreed whole-heartedly. Paul had already thought further. He decided to make a babai beetle trap.

"How will you do that, Paul?"

"I can make a trap by cutting a Coke can in half and then the babai beetle, once in, will not be able to climb out."

"But why would the beetle go there in the first place?"

"I shall put a concoction in the bottom of the can which attracts the babai beetles."

"What attracts the babai beetle?"

"I don't know, but I have eight weeks to find out. I can vary the mixture at the bottom of the can every few days and record when there are more or less beetles to guide us to the perfect concoction."

I liked this idea and saw the brilliance of his plan. "So you are going to make a sort of moth trap for the babai beetle; he will be attracted to something and then get stuck. Are you going to start tomorrow?" Paul smiled.

The idea of successful research into the liquids which would entice a babai beetle to a Coke trap was exciting if Paul could pull it off. No doubt the *Atoll Pioneer* had a few column inches on this important development with anticipated results, although I cannot recall the details. At the time, there were many other matters which preoccupied me.

The days went by quickly. Eight weeks is more than fifty of them. Every evening over dinner I received an update of the beetles. Paul's records were meticulous. The exact ingredients of his various concoctions, the proportion of the mix, and the number of beetles who had found their way in was recorded carefully as every researcher must. The results were sporadic. A few beetles here and there, but never enough to give a clue as to the direction of the trial. Sometimes there was a sudden increase in trapped beetles but a repeat with the same concoction a few days later produced quite different results. Perhaps the babai beetle knew something which Paul didn't.

More days went by. Paul worked ever more frantically and borrowed my sedate Honda every day to visit Reuben's babai pit at dawn and at dusk. I had almost given up, or forgotten, as Paul's last week approached. But, in his last week, I found him in my house with tears in his eyes. "What happened?"

"The tins were full of beetles this morning!" he said, with a grin through the tears.

Being very British and knowing a thing or two about 'reserve', I encouraged him to write everything up meticulously and thoroughly. He nodded sagely. He knew he needed a few more days to complete his research report. A couple of days later, with the writing still unfinished, Paul left Tarawa on the weekly flight to Fiji. I saw him off with a firm handshake and further encouragement to write up his research speedily.

The next few days were quieter. I had forgotten how quiet my evenings had been before Paul had come to stay for three months. Our evening dinners together had been such a delight.

A further week passed before my next visit to Reuben. I mentioned how happy Paul was when he left. Reuben smiled warmly as he told me the village elders often discussed Paul's work as the babai beetle was such a problem for them. They also had another long discussion in the *maneaba* a few nights before Paul left. I wondered what they had talked about.

Reuben replied, "They wanted to give him a reward for all his efforts and dedication. He really tried so hard."

"So, what did they decide to give him?" I asked.

"Well, knowing how hard he tried to fill his tins with beetles, we asked all the children of the village to catch some beetles and to put them in his tins."

A short pause followed. My emotions were rather mixed while realising my need to write a letter to Paul, and quickly. I was wondering how he would take the news when Reuben mentioned the meatier subjects before us, a complete overhaul of the local tax system.

THE CUBAN TRAIN DRIVER

I fell in love with Cuba instantly. This giant crocodile-shaped island has everything: the music; the dance; the scenery; the ancient automobiles that immediately transported me to another era; the smell of cigars and lots of laughter. I wondered why I hadn't been several times already, but was glad to be here now. Somehow my career had taken me almost everywhere in the Caribbean, but I had managed to leave the best till last. In the 1980s, while working for the state sugar industry in Jamaica, I used to imagine Cuba would be just like Jamaica, but very much larger. Ten times larger, actually. But she is much more than that, and quite different.

To enhance my visit, a Cuban man called Liber Frometa was recommended to me. My Spanish was nil; his English was reputed to be perfect. He was a very experienced guide and he had a car. He picked me up from Havana airport with a clear sign showing my name. When he

kindly opened the back door of his car for me, I said, "No, I prefer to be in the front with you." When he asked me for instructions, I quickly pointed out that he knew his homeland infinitely better and suggested he recommend what he would do and why. That would be easier for me. We could discuss and chat. I preferred a guide to be a friend who was open to suggest spontaneous changes to the plan. With Liber this was easy.

Liber told me he had a favourite baseball team 'Industriales' in Havana and they had an important match in three days. So, I said, "Let's go together." We bought tickets for the game before setting off westwards to the beautiful tobacco country in Vinales. The fields reminded me of my earlier experiences in the Caribbean and prompted me to share some of those stories.

Liber was fascinated. During the 1980s, I had not only been responsible for the sugar industry of Jamaica, but also for Belize and Guyana, as well as supporting the industry in Trinidad and St. Kitts. I explained how the fields of sugar cane interested me much more than the factories.

I remembered that Cuba was more than a bigger island. She was the largest sugar grower in the world, producing over seven million tons annually. I asked if we could organise a trip to some sugar cane fields so that I could see their varieties and gauge the way they farmed. Liber had already proposed a visit to the old colonial town of Trinidad on the west coast of Cuba. He suggested that Trinidad would be an ideal place for exploring the nearby sugar cane.

Liber then mentioned that he had an old school friend in Vinales, who he hadn't seen for years. I suggested he invite him to dinner that evening in a restaurant. He was happy, his old friend was surprised, and we all enjoyed the wider ranging conversations. This was a perfect way for me to explore and enjoy a wonderful island with her breath-taking vistas.

When we returned to Havana, I enjoyed my visit to Liber's house, meeting his wife, Madeline, and their two-year old daughter, Sofia. His father challenged me to a game of chess before we went to the baseball game. We had a tense, but ultimately fabulous evening. His team looked to be in a hopeless position but won by striking a

grand slam – a home run with all bases loaded – on the last possible pitch, and I smoked my first ever cigar.

On the morning after the excitement of the baseball win, we drove down towards Trinidad. Of course, we stopped in Santa Clara to see the train wreck and the museum of this decisive battle of the revolution in 1958. I told Liber how "Che Guevara had been one of my heroes as a boy." Liber asked my views of communism. I enjoyed these conversations with my Cuban 'brother'. My travels had taken me to over a hundred and sixty countries, including many communist ones, so I could share some definite virtues which I had noticed. "They don't encourage fundamentalist religions; they generally support a better health and education system and favour equality for women. For me, these are extremely important." After a few seconds of more reflection, I added; "But, what has particularly struck me about Cuba is the absence of envy. I felt that immediately in the way that people treat each other." This was fascinating for both of us as our talking meandered. We talked of capitalism and discussed other faults; the greed, the serfdom, the waste and many other vices. Neither

system was satisfactory.

The town of Trinidad was enchanting: such views of the ocean close by; the hills in the distance and old town squares full of music bands in the evenings. Over a beer, we spoke again about my wish to see the sugar cane fields. Liber suggested that the easiest way was probably for me to take a train from Trinidad. Seeing that I was somewhat surprised, he explained that the train tracks were close to the fields and I would get a much better idea of the lay of the land from the train. Besides, there was not a good road nearby. His idea was to drive me to the railway station in the morning, and then to drive on to a station on the other side of the sugar fields where he would wait for me. This made perfect sense. When he added that the train was an old steam locomotive, my excitement jumped. That would be extraordinary. "What time is the train?" I asked. He thought between 9.00 and 9.30 in the morning. Not wanting to miss it, we decided to have breakfast together and get to the station by 8.30 to be sure.

The following morning, Liber drove with me to the railway station. We arrived early. There seemed to be nobody about. There was a waiting room, however. Inside, a white haired man, probably in his seventies, was sitting with a large book. Being naturally gregarious, I sought to strike up a conversation. His name was Alberto, but he had no more English than I had Spanish. He was happy to show me his book; a photograph album of steam engines. I sat beside him while Liber translated from his bench on the other side of the waiting room. This was odd, but amusing. Alberto and I were close as we turned the pages; we spoke in our own languages while Liber's translation for each of us bounced back like an echo. I asked Alberto the significance of the pictures; he explained that he was a train driver and that these were all trains he had driven over the years.

This was heavenly. I was reminded of my childhood train set, and the stories of Thomas the Tank Engine came to life. Liber must have thought I was in a candy store, watching my delight from the other side of the hall as he translated every detail.

We learned that my train would depart at about 9.15. "Is he going to drive the

train?" I asked. Sadly, Alberto told us that the steam train had broken down and was not coming today. Instead there would be a Russian diesel locomotive with a different driver.

"That is such a pity. I was going to ask you if you would let me ride on the footplate with you." He showed his regret, and I continued, "Would you be willing to introduce me to the driver of the Russian train and ask if I could ride with him?" This idea gave him great pleasure and he agreed at once. We moved out of the waiting room and Alberto took us to the spot where the engine would draw in. There was not a platform as such, just an area where the train would stop and we would climb up

from the grass. Many passengers had arrived to wait for the train and were all milling about on both sides of the track. The diesel locomotive came a few minutes later and Alberto went to speak to the driver. Seconds later, he beckoned me over and I climbed into the cab.

The driver did not speak English either, but we managed with sign language and he indicated that I should sit in the seat on his left. Behind him was a drinks cabinet and he offered me a beer. As we started to move along, I became fascinated by the controls. Clearly the large wheel was not to steer but to regulate speed. I watched him like a hawk and he gestured what he was doing so I could see what everything controlled. There were two brakes, one for the carriages and one for the locomotive. From the way he gesticulated with his hands, I learned that I had to brake the carriages first, before braking the locomotive. An image of my motorcycle in the Gilbert Islands came to mind, remembering the importance of applying the rear brake first and then the front brake so I didn't go head over heels. I imagined the train was similar except that the carriages would just shunt into the train

if not braked first. He then explained how the signs beside the track indicated when the horn had to be used. I expressed my joy and no doubt gave the impression that I had taken in all in.

He stood up quickly and motioned for me to take his seat, which surprised me. I slid in easily and he stood by my left shoulder, watching. Approaching a corner a little too fast he beckoned me urgently to slow down. After the corner, I was encouraged to speed up as if I must be driving too sedately. I forgot to sound the horn in time and was reminded. He seemed to be enjoying my apparent ease with the controls as well as my excitement and soon he made no more gestures. Obviously he approved.

We went over a bridge and, having been alarmed by how close we were to the bridge struts, I had an urge to duck my head before reminding myself that the train must have been over this bridge many times and there would be a sufficient gap. The dimensions must be alright.

As the bridge passed behind us, I looked left and the driver had vanished. My heart jumped. He must have left the

locomotive to go back to the train for something. I hoped he would come back quickly. I noticed the track ahead looked covered in grass. Were the rails still there?

Everything else disappeared from my mind apart from concentrating on the track ahead. Of course I was very worried, but not about myself. The train was full of passengers, and there were places where a village road crossed with children waiting, or watching. There were cows very close to

the tracks with no fencing. I blasted the horn with fury, not wanting to have responsibility for a dead cow, remembering they all belonged to the Government of Cuba. An anticipatory flash of being imprisoned for reducing the Government livestock crossed my mind.

A corner approached and the track started to decline a little, but I had no idea what was beyond the trees. I could not see anything after the corner, like driving up to

the brow of a hill in a car and wondering if the road is straight afterwards. I knew I would not need to steer, that was one dimension less. But, should I slow right down? Or just a little? What could be coming around the corner? My driving instructor had not returned. I would have to be careful as this lack of knowledge of the route was starting to weigh on me; on the other hand, I couldn't give in to the situation and just creep along nervously. The passengers had clearly no idea that the train had no proper driver.

The corner came and went. More cows and more horn blasts. Phew, the train almost scraped them. But, suddenly I began to wonder about the next station. How much further? How much should I slow down to be aligned with the platform, if there was one? This felt like skiing when everything else leaves the mind to focus on staying alive during the descent – I wasn't really in control and only had the merest notion of what I was doing.

Suddenly, I saw a station building and some traffic and knew I would need to slow down soon. Twenty minutes had passed and my driver was still missing. As the station approached he suddenly reappeared. He guided me on the speed necessary to align with the platform. His return was such a relief that my thanks to him were quite gushing.

As I got down from the engine, my legs were shaking. Liber found me. He asked how the sugar cane was. I told him I had forgotten to look. I had been too busy driving the train. He looked at me rather quizzically.

"Please can you help me by translating some questions I have for the driver?"

"Of course." Liber replied, as we both climbed back into the cab.

"Can you ask him where the emergency brake is?" Liber asked and then explained that a lever, which he indicated, would dump a ton of sand under the locomotive and stop the train at once.

"Thank you, that's very interesting but I would like to have known that before driving the train." Liber was starting to wonder what had been going on. I continued, "Can you ask him if he often lets someone else drive the train?"

Liber checked and replied, "No, never… he has never let anybody else drive the train."

"Then why did he let me drive?"

A pause, and then, "He says you are a friend of his friend so he thought you were a train driver."

I was glad to be back in Liber's car, and did not offer to drive as we continued my exploration of Cuba.

THE BUSHMAN, THE DRESS AND THAT TYRE

I cannot say that my visit to Botswana was an accident, but a week earlier this idea hadn't been on my mind. A couple of months before, I had agreed to travel to Rosslyn, near Johannesburg, at the request of Julian, an American client, to review the performance of a factory with him. Since the journey from Chicago to South Africa was long, and the flight cost disproportionate to the length of our visit, I purchased a non-refundable cheaper fare. Unfortunately, six days before we were due to fly, Julian emailed me to say he was sick and we would have to postpone the trip.

Julian offered to reimburse my flight costs. In that instant, I realised how much I was looking forward to being back in Africa, and there would be a 'hole' in my diary otherwise. I emailed him back, saying that I wished him a speedy recovery but he did not need to reimburse me. I would use the ticket and take a break in Southern Africa. That was how the long overdue visit to Botswana came about, one of the most peaceful of the African nations and gateway to the Kalahari Desert.

My energy surged with the prospect of another adventure. The internet offered a variety of local travel agencies, including some that resembled the No. 1 Ladies' Detective Agency of Precious Ramotswe. I chanced upon another simple website and filled in their online enquiry form. Meanwhile, finding a flight from Johannesburg to Gaborone, the capital of Botswana, was easy. There were eight flights a day to choose from for the fifty-five minute journey. Selecting which flight to take took longer than the time to buy a ticket. I paused to have a cup of coffee, savouring the smell of the roasted beans when the phone rang. The number on the screen looked very strange and foreign. Who could this be?

A gentleman by the name of Mr Rowlands was calling in response to my online enquiry. He was a retired primary school teacher and sounded like he had his feet on the ground. The travel agency was his, he explained, and he thought to telephone as my planned visit was in a few days. I thanked him for taking the trouble to call. He confirmed that he could organise a trip for next week and had a driver available. He asked me, "What do you want to do?"

I was stumped for words. Without thinking, I said, "I haven't thought about it." The silence on the line was awkward. I realised he must be taking me for an incompetent tourist who didn't have a clue. That was not the way my Botswana adventure was supposed to start. Then I felt guilty that I was wasting his money on such a long distance call.

He broke the silence by asking, "What about a game safari?"

His question brought me to life. "Well, I used to farm in much of Southern Africa and was hoping for something different. Maybe something uniquely related to the local Tswana culture." I felt relieved; his impression of me must have changed.

"What about walking with Bushmen?" he offered.

"Perfect, I couldn't think of a better idea."

Mr Rowlands promised to find out if any of the Bushmen he knew were available and to let me know very soon. He said that a day or two might be necessary to raise them 'on the bush telegraph'. Two days later he emailed to say that all was confirmed. He had reserved a room at Kgale Lodge in Gaborone. His driver, Tich Mutanga, would collect me at 7.30 the day after my arrival to take me to the Kalahari. There, a Bushman by the name of Size would show me how to survive in the desert. Tich would wait for me in the lobby. I asked for one change to the plan. Would Tich join me for a cooked breakfast at 7.00 so that we could meet properly face-to-face before our long drive side-by-side? Mr Rowlands responded that this would be very well received, and I was pleased that he understood my respect for local guides.

One of my favourite expressions from the Dagara tribe is, "When death finds you, make sure it finds you alive." Just three mornings later, there we were sitting down to a full English breakfast of eggs, sausages, bacon and beans with plenty of toast and coffee. Chatting with Tich was easy. We made an immediate connection and trusted each other. Soon we decided to go.

Tich walked me out to his agency's four-wheel drive Land Cruiser in the classic camel colour. Suddenly, I noticed how unprepared I was. My rolling luggage bag was better suited to airport walks. What was I thinking in taking my laptop in a knapsack to the Kalahari? Climbing into the passenger seat, I noticed the odometer - 350,047 - and even though these were kilometres, this was not a young camel. As we pulled out of the parking lot, the Toyota squeaked. Perhaps the ride would be quieter on sand; my mind was already wandering.

Tich said we had about a hundred kilometres to drive on a tarmac road, and then another hundred and twenty on sand or stones. My knapsack and computer would soon be full of sand. I asked Tich if we could stop somewhere, before the end of the tarmac road, where we could buy a plastic bag, or a sealable container of some kind.

About an hour later, we approached a village with a modest general store. There was nothing suitable to protect my laptop. Instead, we packed a cardboard box full of fresh fruit, including some very juicy South African plums. Tich mentioned there was a Chinese store nearby. We could also try there. We did, with no better luck. But, looking upwards suddenly, I saw high on the wall some rolls of beautiful and colourful cloth for making clothes.

"Tich, do you still have phone signal?" I asked.

"Yes."

"Can you call your wife and ask her how much material she needs to make a dress?"

He looked at me quizzically but made the call. "Three and a half metres," was the reply.

"Right, now can you choose the material your wife will like best?" I insisted.

Having bought the colourful material, I swaddled my laptop and electronics carefully in the middle of the cloth as if binding an Egyptian Mummy.

We set off again and I was a much happier man. I had resolved my problem the African way, by going with the flow. My enthusiasm was infectious although Tich was still a little puzzled.

"Ladies don't think like us, Tich." I laughed. "We think they want a big gift, but they prefer lots of little ones, and we just bought her seven."

"Where are the seven gifts?"

"The first gift: you called, so you were thinking about her. The second, you were thinking of her in a new dress…"

"That's the same gift," he said.

"No, Tich, Ladies don't usually think like that. These are two separate gifts for her. Third, you asked *her* how much cloth she needs for a dress, that's another gift." Tich smiled. "Then you chose the material and that's the fourth. She will be wondering now what this new dress will look like; her wondering is a fifth gift because she doesn't know but she will think more. The sixth is how she will imagine you carefully looking after the material until you see her again, and finally the seventh gift is the anticipation of the surprise when she receives the material."

"Yes, but she will have to make the dress," he said.

"I know, but she will have all the gifts again while her sewing machine is humming. I am sure of it. You will see. And I am happy too, thinking of all this. Of course, there is the bonus that her dress will meanwhile protect my laptop in the Kalahari." Tich smiled again. He said that I wasn't a normal tourist. I didn't mind that, asking him the last time he bought his wife some material for a dress. He understood my point.

We were now off the tarmac road and our banter continued for the next twenty minutes or so. Meanwhile, the Toyota Land Cruiser was being thrown about on the sand and stones like a ship in a storm. The dust and sand were everywhere. Suddenly Tich became silent. I looked at him anxiously. He said, "We have a problem with a rear tyre."

It wasn't just a puncture; the rear passenger-side tyre was shredded. A six-inch nail had gone right through to the rim of the wheel. "Do you have a spare?" I asked nonchalantly to disguise any anxiety. He had. That was a relief, and Tich climbed onto the roof to unbolt the spare before passing the wheel down to me. The solution seemed simple enough; we just had to jack up the vehicle and then remove the nuts holding our damaged wheel. Except there was a lock-nut; the kind designed to stop others from stealing the wheels, and this nut was more than very effective in deterring us. The 'key' spun on the inside and none of our tools could get a grip on the outside. We tried everything. I lay on the ground to push with my legs to give Tich more leverage and pressure on the wrench, but nothing took hold. We were defeated.

There was nothing to do except wait, in the African way, for another vehicle to come by. At least we had plenty of water, and even fresh fruit if needed. Two trucks came after half an hour, but their tools were no better than ours. Forty minutes later, a car came with a young South African couple. The boy, in his twenties, jumped out and looked. "Yes, I have a tool for that." His wrench was designed with a progressive grip and did the trick. We had 'broken the code' of the lock-nut and got the wheel off. But, the new tyre was fixed with only five of the six bolts since we could not use the broken lock-nut again.

Tich was quiet. He looked worried. Was he worried that we no longer had a spare? Or was that my worry? I could have just asked him directly, but respected his silence. Then, I remembered, particularly in Africa, how a vehicle's owner would often expect his driver to pay for a damaged tyre. "How much will a new tyre cost, Tich?" I asked.

He answered, "Three months' wages."

His answer said everything. I replied, "A six-inch nail was not your fault."

"Yes, but I should have stopped sooner. Then the tyre would have been repairable."

I saw his point. I could picture the scene with Rowlands. The shouting and screaming, and Tich having to take a beating, no arguing or he would lose his job.

I didn't feel much better. My entire journey in Botswana would be ruined if Tich suffered because of this tyre. I pledged that I would take care of this somehow. Tich was not reassured. He hardly knew me, why should he take my word?

During the next hour, we spoke less and watched the views more. The laughter and love of his wife's dress had evaporated.

It was mid-afternoon before we arrived at our lodge. The manageress brought us a very late lunch with a beer. With the coffee, she casually announced that there were lion on the salt flats just twenty kilometres away. I didn't want to ask Tich to drive further. But, when I told her we now lacked a spare tyre, she offered their own lodge Landrover and driver. Tich and I looked at each other; there is something about lion. One can never see too many of them.

The lodge driver knew exactly where the salt flats were. We were less than a kilometre from the lion when, suddenly, the wheels of the Landrover lost their grip and started to slip in the sand. Our driver jumped out and immediately took his shovel to dig out the wheels. But, when starting the engine again, the wheels sank deeper. We had another ninety minutes of light left at most. We needed branches, strong twigs or anything we could lay down to make the ground firmer and to help the wheels get a grip. But the Landrover sank even further until the chassis of our vehicle was resting her belly on the sand. The wheels were just hanging there, spinning uselessly.

"Does anybody have a mobile with any signal?" I asked. I certainly didn't, nor did the driver, but Tich had one out of the five bars on his screen. Not enough to make a call we found. We sat in our open Landrover, waiting and thinking. We discussed our options. Walking back would probably take us four or five hours. Maybe we should stay in our open vehicle overnight and walk in the very early morning.

Just five minutes later, another vehicle was heading directly toward us. They stopped and seven strong men jumped out. Their uniforms announced they were research rangers of the Kalahari National Park.

"What are you doing here?" one asked.

"We are stuck."

"No, you are not stuck. You just need a good push." Together we pushed our Landrover out of the soft sand onto firmer ground. What a relief!

They told us the lion were just around the corner and the ground was good so we really should make the most of the last fifteen minutes of light. We saw the lion in the twilight.

Dinner that night was excellent and the beer so refreshing; we laughed about our day's adventures.

Yet Tich was still worried about Rowlands and the tyre. Since we were 'in this together', I suggested that Tich should warn him of the truth. That would soften the blow when the full story came out. Tich did as advised, but clearly was still apprehensive about the final outcome. "Let's sleep on it," I suggested.

The following morning was bright and sunny and the air was deliciously fresh. After an early breakfast we drove to meet Size.

The moment we arrived in the village, I felt as if I had walked through a veil to another world. There are times when I meet indigenous people who are so much at home with nature, and at home with themselves, that there is no option but to relax. I felt at home here.

The children loved the juicy mauve plums. As soon as they took a bite, the juice squirted out and ran down their chins, only to be rescued in their small hands without missing a drop. They giggled with the utmost enjoyment. Their delight brought me back to the dress of Tich's wife.

With a lovely energy, we set off on our 'walk' led by our Bushmen guides. Size walked with a deep connection to the ground, as if the ground bowed beneath each footstep. I saw he was completely in harmony. He would nod to each plant as he passed, sometimes stopping to explain their particular use. Some were for nourishment, others for medicinal purposes. The plant that interested me most was apparently for drinking. I could not imagine how one could drink from such a small leaf. Size proceeded to show me.

Size began by loosening the sand under the leaf with his fingers to find the plant stem. Then, very carefully, he loosened the sand around the stem deeper and deeper into the ground, using his fingers together with a stick which he carried. This was not a quick process as the plant stem had to be preserved undamaged, he explained. As he continued, he seemed to be losing his arm. "The drink will be at the very end of my arm's reach," he said. Having found a tuber, he needed to dig a little deeper to ensure he also released any fine hair roots underneath. Slowly he brought the entire plant and root up to the surface. Some of these 'drinking

plants' looked like potatoes and others like fat carrots. The best for drinking were the potato variety.

With a small knife, Size cut off one side of the potato, as if he had 'removed the left flank' but preserved the vertical stem and other half of the root. Then he put the entire plant back, gently reversing the excavation process he had used. The hole he had dug was backfilled with the same sandy soil. Finally, the leaf was left sitting on the surface just as the plant was when he began. He said everything would grow again and 'repair' the part he had removed. He was like a magician, except that I had missed the drinking part. That was his next trick. He cut up the half potato and squeezed tightly in his hands to drink. There was a lot more juice than the plums I had brought.

I marvelled at his delicate respect for nature. That he could drink and then restore to the ground enough of the plant to leave a 'well' for others. A Bushman would see a plant leaf which had been recently 'tapped' by the evidence on the ground. I regretted my culture's lack of relationship with nature. The thought was painful.

Size taught me how to make string from the aloe plant, but this was more familiar. The way the fibres were rolled on our skin was just the same way the Gilbertese made their string from coconut fibre in the Central Pacific. But the string's use was quite different. Size made a snare with the assistance of a springy sapling, a rabbit's favourite berries and a string noose. The idea was that a rabbit would eat the berries, dislodge some twigs and set off the noose which would tighten around him. Mine went off too quickly and almost snared Size. He roared with laughter.

In the afternoon, Size stopped me and held my arm. "See that print, that's a hyena." I smiled and hugged him. "You know," I said, "There is something about you which is so safe and reassuring. I am so grateful to be walking with you; your spear; bow and arrow, instead of relying on a wretched vehicle." He knew what I meant.

Size was the highlight of my trip to Botswana.

After the day's walk with nature, we spent a last night in the lodge before setting off for Gaborone the following morning. I wanted to share the driving. At first Tich protested, but I persuaded him that the drive was long and tiring; also that I was no stranger to driving in Africa.

I had my hands on the wheel as we approached Gaborone in the late afternoon. I had to wake Tich to find the way to my hotel. After unwrapping the laptop packaging, we shook the cloth to remove all traces of sand before refolding the beautiful design carefully. I looked forward to meeting Tich at breakfast the next day. We were going to visit the highlights around Gaborone, and take a trip out of town to see David Livingstone's mission at Kumakwane.

But, the following morning, Tich didn't come. Mr Rowlands arrived instead. This surprised me, and I wondered why I had not been warned. Rowlands didn't look comfortable as we spoke over breakfast. "Is this about the tyre?" I asked. Rowlands shifted his weight rather uncomfortably. I continued, "Tich is a fabulous driver. I have had an excellent trip with him. We have

enjoyed great conversations, and there is nothing he could have done about that nail in the rocky ground."

Rowlands said, "But he wrecked the entire tyre."

"No; the nail wrecked the tyre. You must know the section of ground just after the end of the tarmac road. You are very lucky indeed to have Tich on your staff. Let me be blunt with you. If I have the slightest idea that Tich will suffer consequences for this, I will regret having come to Botswana." Just in case he was going to resist, I added, "And really, you could take some responsibility for the hour and a half in the sun we had to wait to remove the lock-nut. That has nothing to do with Tich."

"Do you want Tich to drive you today then?" Rowlands asked.

"Well, why don't we three all go together? I know you are free as you have just offered, and I know Tich is free." I had already learned during the previous days

that Rowlands' travel agency consisted of himself, the vehicle and Tich. There was nobody else, but there was no need to share this information.

Rowlands could not disagree and seemed content with that. He telephoned Tich and asked him to come over. We hadn't finished breakfast, so Tich joined us. Before we left the table, and speaking in front of both of them, I said to Rowlands, "I had a really good adventure. We had some challenging moments but Tich handled them brilliantly. I am going to give your agency a tip. I am going to pay for that tyre myself. That will be the end of it."

All was well as we toured the villages around Gaborone together. Having a lovely picnic under the tree where David Livingstone taught, I suddenly remembered my laptop protection. "How was the cloth, Tich?"

His eyes lit up, "Better than my wedding night."

K, Where Are You?

There was quite a melee and a squeeze at the border this morning – peak rush hour with an immigration hall full of impatient and busy travellers. I wasn't in a hurry though; I only wanted to maintain my place in the flow so that others who pushed rather more firmly didn't overtake me. There were just four immigration officers and we were all jostling for position as a funnel eventually narrowed us into neat lines. Which line would be quickest? Luckily, the immigration officers were all fast and efficient, stamping every passport after a cursory glance. No visas are required here. Emerging from the customs hall, I walked past a few stalls selling fruit and water to where Stas was waiting with his smart jeep.

Before making this trip a friend had strongly recommended Stas to me. He was apparently an excellent driver. I quickly discovered he was much more than that. He loved his homeland and was an exceptional

guide. He was also a mechanic. This was reassuring if we broke down far off track. He also had a great sense of humour; this was going to be a relaxing trip.

The scenery surprised me. I wondered where I was. Of course I knew, but hadn't expected these views.

We paused for lunch at a restaurant on the lakeshore. Each table was a miniature pontoon in the lake. Like a small floating balcony with elegant mahogany balustrade, an octagonal roof festooned with royal blue and yellow cloth. The waiter's boat arrived to take our orders before rowing back with each course.

Over lunch, enjoying the breeze, I said to Stas, "If my friends were looking at my photographs now, and wondering where I am, they would say Switzerland without a doubt." He laughed. We imagined playing a guessing game with the photographs and views. I invented an imagined reply to friends. "I must agree; this journey sometimes feels like an Alpine stroll. The two nations have much in common. Their highest mountains are still covered in snow, even in August. Their vast blue lake, with willow trees along the shore and tidy poplars by the road. Are they poplars? I am not sure, but they look as though they could be, with leaves that turn their fair side to face the breeze and whistle or rustle in the wind. Perhaps the rose looks cultivated by the Swiss, but here she is native and growing in the wild. Maybe this is where the rose was born, with colours contrasting from deep majestic purple to vibrant peachy orange. Both nations share many other flowers, bright and inviting in the gentle mountain air."

"There are other similarities; she is also a mountainous and landlocked nation, nestling with some much larger neighbours. There are peaceful valleys with contented cows grazing as if on a Swiss postcard."

"When I crossed the border, the immigration department was quicker than Geneva, just a passport stamp in seconds and no visa required. But, unlike Switzerland, all her neighbours require a visa – there's a clue. She is also like a haven in the mountains." Stas smiled as I continued my commentary.

"The temperature feels like an Alpine summer but the average elevation of just over 9,000 feet is double that of Switzerland, so you will need another guess."

I suggested to Stas that they might guess Andorra next, and I would reply: "Why, an inspired guess. Were you thinking of altitude? The elevation is certainly nearer the mark; and rushing mountain streams beside un-made roads remind me of Andorran villages. Yes, and in the valleys, where the snow has melted; the sheep and cows enjoy the grass, they look quite Andorran."

"We went a little further along the road. The fresh fruit stalls are overflowing with abundance; apples, plums, water melons the size of giant footballs, and buckets of plump-cheeked cherries. Rows of white and yellow fish from the lake hang on frames."

Stas thought they would need more clues.

"Their sapphire blue mountain lake is one of the highest and largest in the world, at an elevation of 5,000 feet. This is where the local fish come from. The lake is 180 km long and 60 km wide, that's ten times the area of Lake Geneva, the largest Swiss lake and this one is twice as deep; one of the deepest in the world, actually."

We stopped our drive for a swim in the lake. Driving onwards, we remembered our game and the extra clues. "I have been in the lake. The water is so warm, like a bath which was once too hot but then the phone rang, a short call just giving time enough for the water to cool to a pleasant temperature."

"There are a few hot springs nearby and their water flows constantly into the lake. Like one of those wonderful hot baths where we adjust the hot water tap with a big toe to keep a trickle of hot water flowing in so we don't chill. Well, this is an endorheic lake, which means there are no outflow rivers. There are 118 rivers flowing in from the surrounding mountains but no rivers flowing out. The water can only escape through evaporation."

Stas added that the Chinese name for this lake is 'hot sea', but then they would guess China and we would have to encourage them to think again. Stas told me more about the lake, so I could give additional clues.

"There is something more interesting about the lake. Archaeologists have discovered a 2,500 year old advanced civilisation with a city, halfway down, and under a thousand feet of water. There is a city wall about 500 metres long, all the way down there. Perhaps this was an ancient valley where a river flowed beside the city before an earthquake blocked the river's way out. The valley then filled up like a bath when they couldn't get the plug out."

We decided perhaps some clues about the people might help. I continued, "The people are so wonderful, friendly and bright. Perhaps, some of the beauty and abundance of their land flows through them. When nature is so generous, one is obliged to give more to others."

"We stopped to talk to a young boy. He has an eagle that looked big enough to lift him off the ground and fly him to school. The children ride horses so young; some look as if they were riding before they could walk."

I suggested to Stas that they might guess Tibet and I would have to reply; "Well, I wonder if there may be such a large high lake over there, but there is not much Buddhism here. There are some other similarities between these lands and Tibet; they share something else though, something very close and much larger."

Stas stopped at a store he knew to buy some provisions for a snack in the hills. He told me that the people we were likely to meet would love these snacks. His jeep had four-wheel drive and bounded up the mountain like a goat towards some small lakes. The family we met were delighted with his tasty picnic supplies. We were invited inside their homes.

We went down a valley to see the broken-heart rock where many eagles hovered.

We drove into a valley with the largest walnut forest in the world, apparently.

Because everyone had been so generous with us, we felt we should be more generous with our clues; a few hints even. In the mountains we were invited into some of the yurts.

Stas thought this would make the answer easy now. But, I wondered if they might guess Mongolia and we would have to say; "No, Mongolia has neither the altitude nor the abundance of fresh fruit. Also, this land is much greener."

I carefully mentioned to Stas that his people do not appear 'fundamentally'

Islamic. After all, those skimpy bikinis by the lake could have been in Europe.

Let me tell you where we are, this is the last stop on the great Silk Road before China. Most of the Silk Roads pass through Kyrgyzstan. Her neighbours are China to the east; Kazakhstan to the north, Tajikistan to the south and Uzbekistan to the west.[1]

[1] There is a precise clue in the preface with 'exactly two and a half giant leaps'. Cuba is 102° east of Kiribati. Botswana is 102° east of Cuba. Kyrgyzstan is 51° east of Botswana. Two leaps of 102° and a half leap of 51°.

TEENAGE TRAVELS, THE WEST SIDE OF INDIA

My first major travel began a few weeks after my eighteenth birthday, just after Christmas 1971, when Air India took me on a long spicy flight to New Delhi.

A few years earlier, my father was appointed Dean of Darwin College in Cambridge. This first mixed and uniquely post-graduate college began in Newnham Grange, the family home of the son and grandson of Charles Darwin. When the first four students arrived, my parents invited them to our home for Sunday lunch. A fine graduate from Ceylon, Vikramabahu Karunaratne, or 'Bahu' as he suggested we call him, had come to write a doctorate in plasma physics.

Bahu's wisdom in philosophy and Buddhism interested me much more, as did the tales of his homeland. Although ten years my senior, we were instantly kindred spirits and Bahu is my oldest friend. Darwin College was conveniently on my bicycle route from school, so we continued our conversations frequently.

A couple of years before my university entrance exams, a plan germinated to 'take a year out' to visit India and Ceylon. By then, Darwin College also had some Indian students and a couple came for dinner to suggest places which must be included in my plans. They recommended travel by train; exploring the western half of India on my way down to Ceylon, the eastern half on the way back up, and advised a minimum budget. If careful, six months in India could be managed with the princely sum of ninety pounds, or 1,800 Rupees, they said. Thus excited, I saved this money by working for the Royal Mail in the Christmas holidays and by labouring on building sites – mostly mixing cement for bricklayers – during other school breaks. My budget included a Zenit-E camera and five rolls of Fujifilm, or one photo per day.

In 1971, while revising for University exams, making detailed plans for this trip was very difficult. The Indian subcontinent seemed to be on the verge of war. If I was going to be able to travel at all, this would have to be a very last minute decision.

There had been trouble between East and West Pakistan since Indian independence in 1947. Although the majority of Pakistan's population lived in the East with the Bengali language, the Urdu language of West Pakistan was chosen as the *only* official language by the Federal Government. Nine years later, following the shooting of student demonstrators, the Government finally relented. Even though Karachi and Dhaka are separated by almost 1,500 miles, West Pakistan was not willing to accept proposals for more autonomy in the East.

In March 1971, East Pakistan sought secession. India immediately supported their independence.

By June, the world was awoken to the brutal suppression of the eastern independence movement by Pakistan's army. The UK's *Sunday Times* printed an article 'GENOCIDE' by Anthony Mascaren. He had the courage to stand up and write that West Pakistan's military officers were "determined to cleanse East Pakistan once and for all of the threat of secession, even if it means killing off two million people and ruling the province as a colony for 30 years." India's Prime Minister, Indira Gandhi, told the editor of the *Sunday Times* that this article had shocked her so deeply it set her on *a campaign of personal diplomacy in the European capitals and Moscow to prepare the ground for India's armed intervention.*

The threat of war hung in the air for months. On 3rd December, the Pakistan Air Force launched eleven surprise attacks on Indian targets, including Agra, the location of the Taj Mahal. Their codename for this attack was ominous; 'Operation Chengiz Khan'. India was prepared for war; the Taj Mahal was covered by leaves, branches, straw and black *burlap*, or sackcloth, to avoid her gleaming white dome in the moonlight presenting an easy target.

Luckily, India prevailed before Christmas, East Pakistan obtained her independence as Bangladesh, and my planned visit could begin a few days later. Shortly after landing in New Delhi, I purchased a 4th class railway ticket, with a further half-price student reduction, for less than £9. This allowed me to travel nine thousand miles on Indian trains.

My childhood deafness equipped me in an unexpected way for this adventure. India has such colours, smells, texture and taste, which senses had been enhanced since my infancy. There was no trace of shame or fear of my voice in such a different land with so many languages. I felt more at ease with myself once away from my own culture. A natural open-heartedness to all those I met opened many doors. Also, my instincts taught me whenever a situation should make me wary and guided me to embrace more quickly the situations which were safe; 'deaf-sight' was my guide. Even though far from home, my heart felt nearer as if riding the horse of my nature and trusting the future.

I cannot remember meeting anybody in India who was unkind to me and most were so helpful with guidance. But, sometimes I was pointed in the wrong direction. My instincts told me that my questioner wanted to please me and to receive my gratitude for his guidance, even if he didn't know the way. Once wise to this, the solution was simple. I asked more often. This enabled me to meet more people and have greater enjoyment whilst sharing my gratitude more widely. The choice of direction came from a sense among several guides' suggestions. We all benefitted from the arrangement.

I felt free and happy as this wonderful journey began to unfold from the North of India all the way down to Ceylon. Whenever someone spoke a seemingly unintelligible language, the 'first hearing system' could be relied upon for us to communicate with warm smiles.

The first stop, as recommended by Darwin students, was a visit to the Golden Temple at Amritsar where pilgrims were allowed to stay with free accommodation and food. They also invited me in and made me so welcome without even troubling my modest budget.

After a few days in Amritsar, the train took me back to Delhi. This time, a man invited me to stay with him in the slums; I thought this might be a worthwhile

experience and, with a budget of only three Rupees per day for accommodation, I was keen for economies. But, during the night, I didn't like continually having to kick rats off my sleeping bag.

To save staying another night with rats, I escaped by train south to Agra with her beautiful fort and exquisite Taj Mahal.

Nothing prepared me for the peace and wonder of this mausoleum. There were very few visitors because the *burlap* and branches that disguised her had only just been removed. Sitting in the evening sunlight, my mind was tormented by the contrast between exquisite beauty and the recent traumas suffered by Bangladesh while the Taj Mahal was veiled in *burlap*. Such sadness and suffering alongside.

The onward journey west included Fatehpur Sikri where Emperor Akbar founded his capital of the Mughal Empire in 1571. There is a giant chess set where people performed as the chess pieces and sometimes suffered once 'taken'.

During my visit, the continuity of terror was provided by an artist jumping off the top of the vast entrance gate directly into a small pool which didn't seem either wide or

deep enough to catch him. But he had clearly done this before and repeated his trick for our entertainment and a few coins.

Before leaving home my father implored me to make just one promise. As a veterinary surgeon, he was very anxious about rabies. He asked me, if bitten by a bat, dog or monkey, to immediately come home. The only way to protect against rabies was a three-week course of injections in the stomach which might be very risky in India, he worried. A veterinary friend of his had died of rabies when bitten by a puppy in The Gambia, and the details of his suffering were particularly gruesome. This life saving promise did not seem unreasonable. However, rather sooner than expected, my promise was to be tested.

The train, full of such social company and colourful saris, rattled west to Jaipur with her fascinating Hawa Mahal. This is the Palace of Winds by Maharaja Singh, with many small viewing rooms for each of his wives to enjoy the view without intruding on each other. Nearby, Jaipur also boasts the Jantah Mantar observatory with many astronomical instruments and apparently

took over and I rose up with a roar like a gorilla which surprised everybody in the park, but shocked the monkeys even more and they fled.

My relief was short-lived. The monkeys had left, a small victory, but one of them had bitten me and the earlier promise to my father flooded my mind. I was scared and had to find a doctor at once. Not so easy on a Sunday afternoon. Rushing back into the centre of Jaipur, I asked several people for a doctor and followed their guidance. Their suggestions did not seem right but several suggested an alleyway with a small rickety external staircase. I climbed up onto a roof terrace where four men in vests and sarongs were playing cards. Asking them again where I could find a doctor, one kind man asked what my trouble was. Having explained the story, he put down his cards to ask if he could examine the monkey bite. Trembling somewhat, I explained my fear of rabies. He nodded and thought about it carefully. "I think you are going to be alright. It is true that the monkey has scratched you but your skin is not significantly broken. Rabies is carried in the monkey saliva and you are very lucky here as he bit you in an area where you

the world's largest sundial. I was able to climb into some of the instruments for a better view. After wandering around several of them in a small park, I rested on the grass. Several monkeys were sitting quietly a few yards from me, but causing no concern. Just behind me, a family with small children was having a picnic. The afternoon was pleasant until the children started throwing stones over my shoulders at the monkeys without any provocation. I ducked to avoid their stone throwing which was the wrong response. The monkeys were enraged and jumped shrieking towards the stone-throwing children. But they found me first on their way. Two jumped on my shoulder; one climbed on my back and bit me on the backside. Suddenly, my instincts

are wearing two layers of clothing, your trousers and underpants. My advice would be to do nothing but if you are still worried then you can come tomorrow to my surgery at the Jaipur hospital."

I thanked him and wished them all well with their afternoon. But, in the morning I was still worried. On the other hand, his advice made sense. Also, my adventure in India was so interesting that to give up so early would be a very difficult choice to make. Vacillating between two opposite courses, an easier decision was made to visit

his surgery in the hospital. He looked rather different than the one playing cards on the terrace but was just as kind. Although he had made up his mind not to worry, he saw I was undecided. He suggested taking a break from his hospital work to show me around. We went out to his motorcycle and drove to Amer Hill.

The palace has magnificent silver doors. By the afternoon, my fear of rabies had waned and it was easier to remain in India. From time to time in the following months the thought still troubled me. A memory of

the doctor's patience and generosity in showing me around will always stay with me, as will my guilt for the other patients who had to wait longer or see someone else that afternoon.

After two nights in Jaipur, my railway ticket whisked me to Udaipur with a Maharaja's palace in the centre of a lake. Arriving after lunch and admiring the view, I decided to take a photograph of the city from the far side of the lake. It was easy by bus, they said. Once the bus seemed far enough around, and beginning to veer in the wrong direction, I hopped off and walked twenty minutes or so down to the water. However, once there, my surroundings were quite different from what I had imagined. Just open grass and a few trees, with nobody else to ask which bus to take back. It seemed simpler to just walk around the lakeshore rather than go back over open ground to the road and attempt to find a bus. I guessed the walk along the shore couldn't be more than three miles to get back to town. Probably not much more than an hour's walk. But waiting for sunset was not wise after all. Darkness would make my shoreline return to town alone tricky. As the sun started to wane, I took just one picture as my budget for photographs was equally tight.

Walking along briskly, after a quarter of an hour I came to a very high wall which ran straight into the lake. The wall was several feet higher than the water for fully fifty yards. This seemed very odd. Not knowing what it was or why it was there, I found a tree to climb and look over. The grass and trees seemed the same on the other side. So I found a way to climb over this wall and drop down about fifteen feet onto the grass before continuing my shoreline walk.

Except, about fifteen minutes later I came across another very similar wall, also going down into the lake like before. Since the town was still in full view on my right, in the twilight, I was clearly not lost. There was no choice but to find a way to climb over this wall too, but it was much harder than the first one, even if about the same height. I hoped there were not any more such walls on this obstacle course. Luckily there weren't.

Almost an hour later I arrived in the centre of town and settled in a small stall for rice and lentils, and of course a *garam chai* or hot tea. Others, eating their supper, asked me about my adventures and were fascinated by my tales. I suddenly remembered the climbs on my lake walk and asked the restaurant about these walls which went into the lake. "Oh that's an enclosure where the maharajah kept his tigers," they said.

After Udaipur, I went to Ahmedabad, with her Jhulta Minar or shaking minarets. A boy demonstrated how they worked. We each climbed a different minaret by the spiral staircase to the top deck. He signalled

and at once my minaret floor shook in harmony. We waved and laughed.

I loved the street markets on my way to Bombay and visited the Elephanta caves.

After Bombay, the journey south included Poona, Bangalore, Mysore with her Nandi Bull, and some days in Madurai with her magnificent temples.

I often took advantage of the Railway Retiring Rooms; these consisted of a dormitory for my class of ticket on the upper floor of the station. The bed was clean, the station master always woke me in advance of the next train, and this service did not trouble my budget either. The last train meandered through Manamadurai to Rameswaram where a ferry links India with Talaimannar in Ceylon.

Six months in the Indian subcontinent warrants a whole book, particularly with the generosity and kindness received from so many. Although travelling alone, I was never alone.

CEYLON'S MISGUIDED BUSES

The ferry arrived at Talaimannar on the northwest shore of Ceylon one full moon. Bahu had instructed me, on arrival in Colombo, to pass by the office of his uncle who would look after me in his village until Bahu came down from Kandy to collect me. I hadn't known that his uncle designed stamps. In his office were lovely paintings of Ceylonese scenes. They were shrunk in printing from wall hanging size for the first edition of Sri Lankan stamps when Ceylon changed her name, on 22nd May 1972, a few days after my arrival coincidentally.

Bahu's uncle had a lovely family, two teenage daughters, two sons and a young puppy. They all welcomed me so sweetly and I enjoyed working in the rice fields wearing my sarong. A few days later Bahu turned up. I had just developed a very high fever with bloody diarrhoea and was in extreme pain. He took me at once to a witch doctor in the neighbouring village, an elderly lady who seemed very wise. After translating my symptoms, she collected some ingredients and mixed up a bright red liquid, which had to be drunk at once. Although feeling better immediately, she gave me enough to take for a few days.

The following morning we set off together by bus up to Kandy. Arriving in the central Colombo station from his uncle's village, Bahu suddenly remembered he had forgotten something. "Wait here," he said, "I just need to get something. There are some aunts in my house and I need some poison powder." He said it so calmly, it was odd. Clutching my bottle of red liquid from the witch doctor while waiting, I wondered what else about him I didn't know. But he had said that so normally. It was puzzling and perturbing, making me wonder how to address this awkward subject. On his return, just as calmly, my question was, "How many aunts are there in your house?" He replied, "Hundreds and they are quite big." As he demonstrated their approximate size with his thumb and forefinger, I told him of my relief that he had meant to say ants and he laughed enough to infect the whole bus.

His house was two hundred yards uphill from the Kandy central bus station, and very comfortable. The shower was in the garden with a bucket and rope next to a well. He had a cook who loved to tease me, and many interesting books. Kandy, being in the centre

of Sri Lanka, was perfectly placed for radial daily tours. There were many temples and ancient monuments which were easily accessible by bus. After breakfast, when Bahu set off to teach at the university, I went down to the bus station and selected a bus from the list he made for me.

Except, later that morning, the bus did not go to the destination written on the front. This didn't really matter as the bus went somewhere else which was also on my list. Perhaps the bus driver hadn't set the destination properly, I mused. But, the next morning, the same thing happened. This was clearly not a coincidence. Were the buses in Sri Lanka playing the same tricks on me as directions given in India? It was very intriguing.

Over dinner that evening, even with our logical physics brains, we couldn't make heads or tails of it. Bahu suggested the following morning I find someone who spoke English and asked where the bus was going, never mind what it said on the front. I did. Again they didn't match. My interpreter saw the problem immediately. The bus drivers had a long roll with a list of places to choose from which they wound forwards or backwards with a key until finding their chosen destination.

Each destination was written in Sinhala, Tamil and English, in that order, as shown in this example for Dambulla.

දඹුල්ල
தம்புள்ளை
Dambulla

However, preferring to have Sinhala more prominently placed in the centre of their destination screen, the Tamil underneath was also correct but the English destination (now appearing on top) referred to the previous destination on the roll.

The English destination was therefore guaranteed to be wrong.

Since many drivers could not read English, they hadn't noticed. Since everybody else looked first for either Sinhala or Tamil, they were not troubled. Having learned from a driver how to adjust the roll, my problem was solved. For the next two months, each morning after arriving at the bus station, I would ask a friendly driver to lend me his key and wind the screen destination to put Sinhala on top to see the right destination in all three languages.

The bus drivers got used to my antics and always laughed when they saw me in the mornings. Some probably thought this teenage English boy had a 'quaint habit' of rearranging the face of their bus to see where they were going. It is funny how one's forgotten infancy keeps cropping up as we meander through life. My father told me how, as a toddler, I used to turn his face so that I could read what he was saying during my deaf years. He called this 'quaint' as he didn't yet know I was deaf. Meanwhile, all the drivers at the central bus station made me very welcome. Those 'in the know' explained the reason of my 'quaintness' to other drivers who smiled broadly. A 'hearing person' would be less troubled as they would more naturally ask where the bus was going, and the destination sounds the same in all three languages.

Speaking of Dambulla, I was happy to find a bus that actually went there. The cave monastery is said to be over two millennia old and is the largest, best-preserved cave-temple complex. There are five sanctuaries full of statues. Perhaps the passengers on the bus, or those at the temple, did not know what to make of this solitary teenager, but they all made me feel at home instantly.

From Kandy, it was easy to visit most of the historical sites as well as the beauty of the island in the ensuing weeks. At the weekends Bahu was free to travel with me and we usually went to his uncle's home near Colombo as he was becoming more interested in a political career than lecturing in physics. He saw the need to do more for his country and the repressed in particular. I was happy to hang out with his teenage cousins while he was preoccupied by more serious discussions.

Anuradhapura is the oldest kingdom of Sri Lanka and was a little too far for a day trip, so the bus driver invited me to stay overnight at his home. He had three children and a calf.

The earliest evidence of habitation in this region is around the 10th century BCE and the oldest Buddhist temple, Thuparamaya, dates from the period of King Devanampiya Tissa in the 3rd century BCE.

Looking at the beautiful white stupas reminded me of the stories of Sinbad the sailor in *The Thousand and One Nights*. Sinbad made seven voyages to the Island of the Lion, *Serendib*, and he returned with tales of a mythical bird, the Roc. He never saw this bird but saw the eggs she laid.

I wondered if he was seeing the white stupas and imagining the vastness of the Roc bird which must have laid these 'eggs'.

Speaking of giants, there are some ruins that look like a giant hairbrush pointing to the sky. Closer examination suggests that they might have been stone columns supporting a seven-storey building with wooden floors. Perhaps the building caught fire and the all the columns fell to the ground thus creating the 'giant hairbrush'.

My guide told me that in the late 5th century CE the King of Anuradhapura was Dhatusena. He was overthrown, and 'walled up alive' by his illegitimate son, Kashyapa. The rightful heir, Moggallana, escaped to South India to gather an army to reclaim his throne. Meanwhile, fearing the inevitable return of his half-brother, Kashyapa abandoned Anuradhapura and found a safer location fifty miles south on the top of a rock where he built a palace. The fortress of Sigiriya, decorated with frescoes, must have felt impregnable. The name comes from Sīnhāgiri, or Sanskrit for the Lion Rock.

However, inevitably, Moggallana duly returned in 495 CE and declared war. Kashyapa came down from his rock but his armies abandoned him and he fell on his sword.

The view, while standing almost four hundred metres above the plains on the top of Sigiriya, is extraordinary. Clearly, if he wanted to save himself, Kashyapa should have stayed up there. But, then he might have run out of water and food. Had he thought of that?

The guide took me to caves with inscriptions from the 3rd century BCE

saying they had been donated by Buddhist monks, but the area has been inhabited for thousands of years.

After the adventures at Sigiriya, I made a day trip from Kandy to Polonnaruwa. This city is where the second oldest Sri Lankan kingdom was established by the Hindu Chola dynasty after their invasion of Anuradhapura in the 10th century; a time when the Buddhist way of life in the north of Sri Lanka was destroyed. There is, however, a 14 metre statue of a reclining Buddha which was built there in the 12th century and during the Chola period.

One of my favourite daily trips was to watch the elephants bathe in the Mahaweli River at Katugastota. Everybody enjoyed themselves, just like children throwing water

and sponges in a giant bath; two species having such fun. My 'deaf-sight' savoured the way elephants loved to tease their mahouts with extra sprays.

Bahu knew someone who managed a tea estate near Nuwara Eliya and organised for me to stay with him for a few days. I loved the freshness of the tea country hills and developed a taste for my favourite of all teas, a Broken Orange Pekoe. The owner kindly allowed me to send a crate to Cambridge, which lasted me for several years.

Bahu also had a friend of a friend who was a policeman near Galle and I stayed with him a couple of nights. While he was 'on the beat' at work, I went down to the beach to talk with fishermen and discovered

that the English word 'catamaran' comes from the Tamil 'kattumaram' meaning 'logs tied together'.

During many visits around Kandy, people often suggested that I extend my stay to include the highlight of the year in Sri Lanka, the elephant processions in the Kandy Perahera. "About a hundred elephants will be dressed up for a ritual," they said, somewhat excitedly. The idea was very tempting but, sadly, there would not be enough time. I told them all that there was no doubt I would be back, not just for the Kandy Perahera but also because I loved their island so much. They had made me so welcome, they were so peaceful and generous, the climate and food so delicious, the scenery so green and the culture so rich.

When the time came to leave Sri Lanka, it was very hard to tear myself away.

My journey back to Cambridge began by the return ferry from Talaimannar. Except, this time the ferry was full of Tamils being forced home. An agreement had been made between the two governments to repatriate thousands of Tamils back to India every week. Many of them could not read or write. Sensing that help was at hand, they formed a long queue on the ferry deck asking me to help fill in their immigration forms. This was very sad for both of us as they shared their details. They didn't want to leave where they had been born.

THE EAST SIDE OF INDIA

The ferry docked in Rameswaram to disembark with my sadness of leaving Sri Lanka and the despair of thousands of Tamils ousted from the land of their birth.

I took the train to Mahablipuram with her beautiful sandy beaches, temples built by the Pallava dynasty in the 7th century and enormous carvings of elephants. Many of the sculptures and temples were unfinished leaving me wondering why they stopped. Had they run away? Or was there another cause? This region of Tamil Nadu was well connected with busy Chinese and Roman trade two millennia ago. The earliest temples began as solid rock carvings and later evolved to buildings.

My next stop was Madras where I stayed in the youth hostel. There were only two of us and my company was James, a Mid-Western American, waiting for the ferry to Kuala Lumpur on his way to Australia. We ate some of the fiercest

curries and I learned why Madras is famous for them. Apparently, in the intense summer humidity, it is hard to perspire. The Madras chili seems to break a barrier to make us sweat more without an increase in body heat. Luckily, from the teasing of Bahu's cook, I had learned to negate the sharpness and heat of the chili with a teaspoon of sugar. I had also discovered that a little onion had the same effect on him as the extra chili in my evening meal so there was always the opportunity to tease him back. I missed those lovely weeks in Ceylon.

I then took the longest train journey of 1972 from Madras, a direct train to Calcutta that takes thirty-six hours; two nights and a day. Luckily, my fellow travellers were so interested in my stories that the time passed relatively quickly as each stop brought fresh teas. As one of the few passengers travelling the whole distance, I had a regular change of audience.

My first impression of Calcutta was of British Imperialism; particularly the 1906 monument for Queen Victoria, and St Paul's Cathedral completed in 1847.

Despite all of the white marble in Queen Victoria's memorial, she pales when

compared to the exquisite beauty of the Taj Mahal. Maybe I wasn't supposed to compare.

The hustle and bustle of Calcutta is amazing, everything rushing from the ubiquitous Ambassador taxis to herds of goats, and street vendors for everything.

After my exploration of other Indian religions; Sikhs, Hindus and Buddhists, there was a new religion to explore – Jainism. Bahu had taught me some basic Buddhist principles and I recognised some similarities with Jainism, particularly the focus on looking inside oneself for enlightenment, the absence of an external deity, the belief in non-violence and other similar morality. Perhaps I should not have been surprised. Both Buddhism and Jainism were developed in the 6th century BCE in the region of India between the River Ganges and the Himalayas. Also, both Gautama Buddha and Mahavira were of Royal birth.

My teacher was the Jain Temple of a Million Mirrors or Parashnath. The mirrors and reflections of light were soothing to my mind.

From Calcutta, my journey took me towards the Himalayas. The last phase of my first major journey, up to Nepal and west to Kabul, is told in the next chapter.

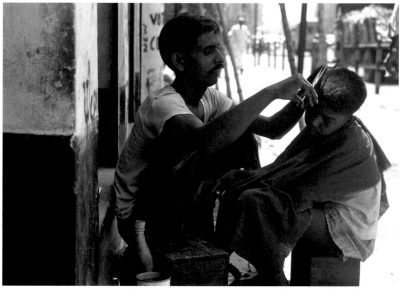

Mini-Skirts in Kabul, Afghanistan

In 1972, after six months travelling around India and Sri Lanka, I took a bus from Patna to Kathmandu in Nepal.

I enjoyed walks in the fresher Himalayan air and treasured my 'trekking permit' issued by his Majesty, King Birendra of Nepal. A free map was included. The lack of contours seemed to suggest the paths were not undulating, but I soon discovered that a 'hill' has to be over fourteen thousand feet to warrant a contour. This explained why I hadn't expected the extent of the daily climbs. Some of the mountain paths were tricky, and some of the bridges nerve-wracking. A three-day trek took me to Nagarkot from where the sun rises directly over Mount Everest, or Sagarmāthā.

The distance from Kathmandu was easy to keep track of though; basic foods cost one Paisa more, or a hundredth of a Rupee, for each extra day of trekking from

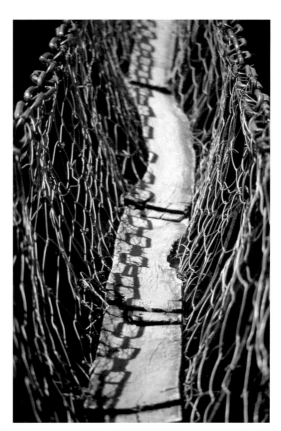

the capital. This compensated for the extra porterage.We were all exhausted by the walks but nobody complained. The villagers were kind and welcoming. And I loved the Nepalese children I met along the way.

Returning to Kathmandu with her distinctive roofs after several days of trekking, I reflected on the enormity of my experience in these wonderful cultures. I was enchanted with the sights, smells, taste and colours but wasn't prepared for such religious diversity. Sikhs, Hindus, Buddhists and Jains welcomed me to their temples and homes. I could not have dreamt of such an adventure.

Now the time had come to plan my way home. My cousin Rowley had taken the 'Hippie trail' to Nepal a couple of years earlier and told me how each city had a favoured haunt for backpackers, like the 'Pudding shop' in Istanbul. He wrote down a list of them for me. These cafés had a noticeboard where we could leave notes affixed with a drawing pin. Some were messages left for a friend; there were warnings of danger; suggestions of good but cheap hotels; advice on transport or good spots to hitchhike; searches for a travelling companion; items for sale or wanted and much else. These 'noticeboards' were updated every day by travellers and created a web of fresh information long before the internet was invented. I wondered if this was the first 'live written guide', although on reflection realised that the Silk Road probably had a version of some kind over two millennia ago.

I never saw myself as a 'hippie', only a backpacker, but accepted gratefully the wisdom of fellow travellers to make my return journey easier. Kathmandu was a favourite destination for 'hippies' and the chosen café was on Freak Street. I found a surprise; a message for me from two school friends who were clearly enjoying themselves. Sadly, they had already left town. I gleaned all the up-to-date information which seemed relevant for my return to London, particularly any advice for a journey across Pakistan, Afghanistan and Iran.

But, before returning home, there was a visit which I had looked forward to for months; Benares, the ancient spiritual capital of India. This city, now called Varanasi, has stood on the banks of the River Ganges for

three millennia and is the holiest of Hindu sites. After a bus from Kathmandu and a train to Benares, there I was.

The city is extraordinary, and the contrast with the Himalayas could not be greater. After sparsely populated mountains, the throngs in small alleyways had a different aliveness. I mingled with the pilgrims and bathed. I took a boat along the River Ganges to explore and paused to watch a funeral pyre. The practice of Sati, or burning a wife on her deceased husband's funeral pyre had been banned for a long time but they told me this still happened sometimes. Such cultural differences made a strong impression on my young mind.

This city is also important in the evolution of Buddha's teaching as he is said to have delivered one of his earliest teachings close by at Sarnath.

From Varanasi, I hoped to catch the Howrah Rajdhani Express which was earning such publicity since her launch in 1969. This new and fast Indian train reduced the journey time to Delhi by almost a quarter, and had air-conditioning. Sadly, such luxury was not permitted with my fourth class student reduction round-India

ticket. Instead, my slower train took twenty-one hours.

A few days later, arriving in Pakistan, I remembered that the 'Hippie trail' notices recommended the train from Lahore to Rawalpindi. From there, a bus was apparently easier to Peshawar. Next, the Freak Street café instructions said the only option was either to hitchhike or take a bus through the Khyber Pass. I decided to take the bus as I was travelling alone and, aged eighteen, not yet battle hardened as a hitchhiker in Afghan border areas. This web of guidance from fellow travellers was priceless.

The views in the Khyber Pass were spectacular, but the Kabul Gorge even more dramatic. Thus I arrived in Afghanistan's capital Kabul and again chose a hotel recommended by fellow travellers.

The following morning, I remember having coffee in a street café outside a branch of Marks and Spencer in Kabul, with girls in mini-skirts. My reader will perhaps imagine that I was hallucinating, or stoned, but this is unfair. Kabul was different all that time ago. In 1972, Afghanistan was still ruled by King

Mohammed Zahir Shah who introduced a democratic constitution including a parliament with free elections, civil rights including rights for women, and universal suffrage.

Back then, there were effectively three irreconcilable societies. The King realised that there was no chance of them ever being reconciled, so he advised them to leave each other alone. Broadly this worked. One section of society was essentially Pashtun; another was the Mujahedeen who believed that they had the right and duty to slit the throats of non-believers; and finally there was a section of society which could have been transplanted from a café on the Champs Elysees in Paris. These extremes of culture could not have been further apart, but there was little sense of discomfort.

I enjoyed the market although the clouds of flies aiming for the meat section were troubling. I purchased an Afghan coat and a curved sword. Along my way, I enjoyed a conversation with an older man. He wanted me to take this photograph, but from the looks that others gave, I sensed that life might be safer with a camera hidden.

From Kabul, the easiest route to Iran is by the southern loop to Kandahar. I arrived there one evening at a small hotel recommended by the Freak Street café. The owner asked me to give him warning before needing a bath so that he could light a log fire to warm the water. We had a chat and, having asked him about other travellers, he told me a group of six European tourists had been there the previous week. Naturally asking where they went, he replied quite casually that some Mujahedeen had come in the night and slit all their throats. Luckily my instincts helped me to determine that he had not approved. He was clearly on my side, but was not in a position to do anything. He had to accept something which could happen to tourists. I decided to trust him as I felt safe with him, although I sensed he needed to appear neutral in mentioning the subject in case he suffered consequences. There was no better choice really, as the alternative would have been to wander around town to see if there was another hotel, thereby drawing more attention to myself. As well as advice from experienced guides, instinct is so valuable.

I didn't have a great night's sleep, though.

At first light, seeing that the owner was up, I asked him to light the fire for my bath. Then, rather quickly, I set off for Herat. I wasn't going to hang around in Kandahar, which was the main area of the Mujahedeen.

After a brief visit to the expansive Mosque and market in Herat, my journey took me westwards and I was captivated by the sight of vast caravans of Bactrian camels near Mashhad in North Eastern Iran.

Three weeks later, I was home.

I went up to Oxford University while still digesting my crash course in the value of Knowledge, Advice and Instincts, together with all the religious differences. My fellow students complained that my sheepskin coat smelled too much in the rain.

A WAY TO JERUSALEM

My grandfather Henry and his twin sister Joan were born in 1890 at Bedford. My grandmother Eva met Henry and Joan in the same class at school as five-year-olds. Joan and Eva were immediately best friends.

Tragically, Joan died when she was sixteen from sleeping sickness.

The loss of his twin sister drove Henry to study Medicine, but he also distinguished himself as a young sprinter. At the age of eighteen he won the school championships for 100 yards before starting to train as a doctor. Although he was selected to run for Britain in the 100 and 200 metres at the 1912 Stockholm Olympics, he declined as he felt his medical service was more important.

At the beginning of the 1st World War, Henry was sent to France as a doctor on the front lines. In the Battle of the Somme he became isolated in a wood and continued, for two days and nights, to treat the wounded under constant German shelling. He was awarded the Military Cross.

A little later, he contracted rheumatic fever and was invalided back to England. Once recovered, he was to be transferred to Egypt and Palestine. Henry was very keen on Eva but, being unsure of her response, held back and was cautious. Luckily, he came to visit Eva's family just before his posting to Palestine. He discovered that the feelings between them were mutual and they were brought together again by their shared grief for Henry's lost twin and Eva's best friend. For the next three years, they wrote to each other.

The letters began during the Arab revolt, just after T.E. Lawrence's capture of Aqaba. Captain Henry had arrived in time to be present at General Allenby's liberation of Jerusalem, as was Lawrence, at the end of 1917. Henry remained in Palestine after the end of the war with responsibility for a hospital. He returned to England in 1920 and married Eva soon after. My mother, Joan, shares her name with Henry's lost twin and Eva's best friend who was so dear to both her parents.

Henry started a medical practice in Norfolk but caught pneumonia and died just two days following the first symptoms, in 1927 when my mother was only four. So, my only knowledge of my grandfather is through his letters to Eva. I regret that we never met as we are, without doubt, kindred spirits. We agree, quite uncannily, on so many issues and *Lawrence of Arabia* is my favourite film.

During 1973, I crossed the Sahel from the Nile at Khartoum to the West Coast of Africa, and then crossed the Sahara by way of Mauritania.[2] The desert tribes were so generous and kind to me. On my return, my

---

[2] This journey is published as *Khartoum to El Aaiun*

grandmother gave me Henry's Arab headdresses in fine silk, two rugs and an inlaid coffee table from Damascus, tea glasses from the market in Jerusalem and a copy of my grandfather's letters. One of the rugs was goats' wool and bore the crest of Guy's Hospital in London where Henry received his medical diplomas in 1913. Armenian refugees had made the rug and I imagined the care they must have felt to have woven this wonderful gift for him. I felt so much at home and close to my grandfather as I decorated my rooms in Oxford with Henry and Eva's memories as I began my second university year.

My first priority was to repay some of my debt for the kindness received during my African journey. All I could offer was free lessons in Mathematics and English to students from Africa and the Middle East. I advertised in the Oxford Mail. Several students came regularly for afternoon tea and tuition. I mentioned that my very modest offer was a wish to repay some of the debt of gratitude for the nomadic hospitality which had sustained me during such a long African journey. They understood immediately.

Among them was a boy my age, Nabhan Al Nimer, who came for the whole academic year. He was from Palestine, the West Bank of Jordan, and a real gentleman. His English was excellent; we had great conversations and enjoyed each other's company. We became good friends and forgot about the free tuition.

Nabhan was fascinated with my grandfather's letters, particularly the description of Palestine in 1917 and a chance to feel silk headdresses worn during the Arab revolt. The following week, Nabhan surprised me with a gift of a Palestinian headdress to add to my collection. He then asked about my plans for the following summer. He suggested I come and visit him in the West Bank. He wrote his name on a little piece of paper, in Arabic, just his name and 'Nablus'. No address or phone number. I can still see that piece of paper now, a little scrap torn out of the exercise book that he brought for his lesson notes; about the size of a playing card.

The idea of visiting Palestine was very appealing. Was this because Nabhan was so charming, or was my grandfather calling me? Were Henry's letters beckoning me? So began my next journey in the summer of 1974 with a flight to Lebanon.

Beirut wasn't calm at all. One evening, returning to my hostel, there was a bullet hole through one of my shirts in the cupboard. That did not seem promising and spurred me to move on quickly to Baalbek and the Temple of Jupiter.

I hitchhiked to Damascus where the markets reminded me of Henry's inlaid table and rugs. Although the market was very lively, otherwise Damascus had an uneasy feel; probably because of the recent war. There were eerie similarities. My grandfather had travelled from Beirut to Baalbek and then Damascus in March 1919, except he went by train. The bullets he had faced were much more frequent and dangerous than the solitary hole in my shirt. I wondered if he was guiding me. After a couple of days there, my wandering took me East to Palmyra.

Much has recently been destroyed by the 'Caliphate of Isis'. This part of the world seems to have never known peace throughout all recorded history.

After the Roman ruins of Jerash, I arrived at Amman in Jordan. The West Bank

was considered part of Jordan. I visited the Jordanian Home Office to apply for a permit. They asked the purpose of my visit to Nablus. "To visit a friend," I replied. They asked whom? Replying, "Nabhan Al Nimer," they told me he wasn't there. Sensing my surprise, they added that he was still in Oxford and he wouldn't be home for another three weeks. They said they would give me a permit then, so I would have to come back later. This was very mysterious, but they had no doubt of where Nabhan was and when he would be home.

Not having a plan apart from the visit to Nablus, I decided to visit Petra. Whilst hitchhiking down there I was given a ride by Paul. He was about my age and was driving a brand new orange Volkswagen Passat which his mother had recently bought. She suggested he drive around for a few months to reduce the Canadian import duty. We travelled together like good friends. I took a picture of him while we climbed the monuments in Petra. We had the place to ourselves, as there were so few tourists in the months after the Yom Kippur War. After more driving around the south of Jordan, and having nothing better to do, we

Climbing the monuments at Petra,
with Paul, for a better view

decided to drive to Kuwait. This seemed a good idea. We thought we would be able to take the car across the Persian Gulf somehow and visit Persepolis and Isfahan, in Iran.

The direct route to Kuwait is straight across the Saudi Desert. We thought, why not? What would you expect of two boys our age with instructions to put mileage on a car with nowhere else to go? So, we went to the Saudi Embassy in Amman to ask for a visa. They told us rather politely that we should come back in the morning for breakfast with the ambassador. So, we simply came back early the next day for our breakfast. Clearly, this was also a first for the ambassador. He was not expecting nineteen or twenty-year-olds who wanted to drive across the desert. He asked what we were up to and we replied, "Just driving around and visiting." This seemed reasonable to him. The visa was prepared by his consul as we chatted over coffee. A warm breakfast had been spread out and served in the nomadic tradition.

Then we asked him how to find our way across the desert. Very casually, as if describing a shop around the corner, he told us to drive north-east in Jordan to a village; the name slips my mind now. Then we should turn right into the desert until we found the Jordanian border guards. After them, we were to turn left towards the North, and after a while we would find the Trans Arabian pipeline. He said we couldn't miss it. We should keep the pipeline on our left all the way to Kuwait. There wasn't a road but the sand alongside was quite firm.

Looking back, maybe this sounds absurd. It was. We were very naïve. We didn't really know what we were doing. We decided to drive mostly at night. We thought we could drive fast and get there in a matter of hours. So, we set off in the early afternoon to make sure we found the pipeline before dark. We measured on the maps and found the drive was just over 750 miles, or something like that. We thought the late afternoon would be cooler and then we could share the driving throughout the night to arrive the following morning in Kuwait. If we averaged 50 miles an hour this would mean arriving in Kuwait before the midday heat. The idea is quite ridiculous, really, looking back. But we thought this was straightforward.

Well, we were completely mad, and very lucky. We didn't even take much spare water as we thought we wouldn't need much at night, or any food for that matter. Everything was fine at first. We found the Saudi border crossing in the village just like the ambassador had said. Soon enough we found the pipeline and we rattled along beside at over sixty miles an hour on firm small stones and sand. But, after a couple of hours, and very suddenly, there was a loud bang and the car just stopped, dead. This felt as if we had hit an invisible wall or concrete block in the ground and the car slammed to a halt. We both jumped out immediately and saw that the back axle had separated from the fixings. The rear wheels and tyres had jammed into the wheel arches and chassis; a complete mess. We were both scared. The car did not look like ever moving again. As bad as a camel that had broken both his hind legs and wouldn't be able to get up or move another inch however hard he scratched with his forelegs. Luckily, this happened before dark.

There weren't any other vehicles around. We didn't see anybody else. We hadn't seen another vehicle since we left

Jordan. Just the empty desert and the comfort of the black pipeline like a giant handrail on our left. At least the direction was clear. The sand next to the pipeline was hardly a busy highway we had learned. We had no idea what to do. Being suddenly so nervous, I needed to pee and walked back three or four yards to relieve myself. At once, I saw a metal bolt in the sand, about six inches long and bent. I picked it up. We decided this must belong to our car. Neither of us were mechanics but we jacked the car up on some stones, freed up the axle and saw where the bolt belonged. It served to fasten a strut from the chassis keeping the axle in the middle of the wheel arches. We were able to hammer the bolt straight and then fix it back in. Just like that.

We found we could drive again. That smile from Paul as the car moved off smoothly will always remain with me. My relief was enveloping. But we were more careful after that. Not as fast as before; we agreed to set a maximum speed of about forty, or less if the ground was bumpy.

We drove in turns while the other slept. The drive was surprisingly calm, although we had to look out for large stones or small rocks among the sand which might jolt the axle and our recent repair-work. Looking keenly for rocks kept the mind occupied. We never saw another car or even a camel all night. As the sun started to rise I felt much safer. There is something about dawn that always rouses the spirits. We found a Saudi well surrounded by camels in the early morning.

We were no longer on our own. The feeling of being back among animals and people was wonderful, a beautiful sight.

Soon after, we found a normal asphalt road with a garage and could fill the car up with gas. That felt good. Even now, I still get a great feeling whenever a car has just been filled to the brim, the same feeling of relief. It's incredible to imagine it now, but the gas was sixpence a gallon. That's about four US cents, so between one and two dollars to fill up the entire tank. When the garage owner saw we were young foreigners he waived the bill entirely. Just imagine that now.

A few hours later, we were in Kuwait. I learned an unforgettable expression.

إذا تعاركت سمكتان في البحر
فلابد أن يكون المسبّب إنجليزي

This means, "If two fish should fight in the sea, it must be caused by the English." Funny, but it's very serious at the same time.

I realise the trouble stirred up around the world by my native land, particularly in the Middle East. This expression has always stuck with me. Often on my journeys, when meeting someone from this part of the world, I write the words again and surprise them. I enjoy their amusement while sharing my embarrassment, combined with the irony of an Englishman writing this down for them.

More than just sometimes, we English provoked a fight surreptitiously and then just stood there with a stiff upper lip and a pith helmet looking as if this was nothing to do with us. Perhaps we were just waiting for the fighters to ask us to be the referee as they were unaware of how we had provoked the problem to start with. My nation has seemingly been 'poaching and game-keeping' all over the place.

We went down to Kuwait port and quickly found a dhow that was willing to sail with our car across the Persian Gulf to Khorramshahr in Iran. Then, we drove on to visit the wonderful Persian history and culture at Persepolis and Isfahan.

Whilst in Isfahan, I suddenly decided to go back to see if I could find Nabhan in Nablus. I wasn't giving up that easily. Or, was something else guiding me? But, I wasn't going to cross the Saudi Desert again.

I left Paul with his car and hitchhiked alone to Teheran. Then I continued west to the middle of Turkey before turning south towards Damascus and crossing Syria a second time.

I enjoyed my pause in Hama to watch the children swim by the giant wheels.

Arriving back in Amman two weeks later, I went immediately to the Jordanian Home Office to ask again for a permit. They asked the same questions. Why did I want to go there? I said, "To visit a friend." "Who?" "Nabhan Al Nimer." But this time they replied: "Well, that's all right then. We will give you a permit." And they gave me the permit without any more questions. I wondered how they knew about Nabhan. This was intriguing and very mysterious.

I took a bus to the Allenby Bridge over the River Jordan to the West Bank. The border crossing was gruelling but of a different kind. The Israeli officers went through everything. Even a bar of soap was cut in half to see what was inside. Luckily, not having much personal luggage, this didn't take too long. So, after that, I caught a bus to Nablus. On the bus, I wondered if

I would find him. Or even how to begin looking.

As I got down, I asked the first person I met, a young woman, if she could please help me find where Nabhan Al Nimer lived. I showed her the little piece of paper, but there was no need as she spoke excellent English. She said, "Yes! I will show you," and sounded as if she was certain. So we walked together and after a few blocks she pointed out his house. Knocking on the door, there he was. A relief after all my adventures and a very welcome rest with iced lemonade.

Nabhan loved the story of my adventures. But, remembering the conversations in the Home Office in Amman, I asked him how everybody knew where he was. Rather sheepishly and humbly, he said: "Oh, my aunt is the Queen of Jordan. Queen Alia."[3]

[3] I subsequently learned that Nabhan's grandmother and Queen Alia's father are both from the Toukan family.

THE STANS

The Persian word for 'country' or 'place' is 'stan' and is written as ستان

The Proto Indo-European ancestor of stan is the source of the English verb 'stand'.

The globe shown here, from Wikipedia, shows the lands with 'stan' as a suffix to their name in dark green. The lighter green territories sometimes use this word internally, and regionally, but not in their country name. India was known to the Persians as Hindustan.

The globe shows rather clearly that the way from China to the Middle East or Europe has to pass through at least one, if not several, of 'The Stans'. A common route of The Silk Road skirts the Taklimakan Desert to Kashgar in China, climbs the Irkeshtam Pass into Kyrgyzstan, crosses the Fergana Valley and weaves through Uzbekistan's fine ancient cities of Samarkand and Bukhara, trundles across the

Karakum Desert, pauses at the Oasis of Merv, and continues to Mashhad in Iran before the markets of Baghdad or Istanbul. The next page, in the story of Uzbek Ancestry, shows the location of most of these major cities

My experiences of the 'stans' began with Pakistan and Afghanistan as an eighteen-year-old in 1972. Over many years and a dozen journeys my wanderings took me through the others. There are seven 'stans' according to Wikipedia.

Other 'stans' can be found nestling, but not yet hatched, inside bigger nations. For example, Karakalpakstan is a sovereign nation, with her own parliament, on the Northwest side of Uzbekistan. According to the constitution of Uzbekistan, *"The Republic of Karakalpakstan shall have the right to secede from the Republic of Uzbekistan on the basis of a nationwide referendum held by the people of Karakalpakstan."* We shall see if, and when, this might happen.

The table below outlines the size, population and population density per square kilometre of the 'stans'.

Country	Area km2	Population	Pop/km2
Afghanistan	652,230	31,575,000	43.5
Kazakhstan	2,724,900	18,312,000	6.3
Kyrgyzstan	199,900	6,020,000	27.8
Pakistan	796,095	212,745,000	226.6
Tajikistan	143,100	9,050,000	55.9
Turkmenistan	488,100	5,660,000	10.5
Uzbekistan*	447,400	33,250,000	67.5
*including Karakalpakstan	166,600	1,818,000	11.3

UZBEK ANCESTRY

On my first visit to Uzbekistan, I was introduced to an exceptional guide called Nadya. Everyone said she was so knowledgeable and helpful that one couldn't find better. I could not disagree; all the arrangements were perfect as we passed through Tashkent, Samarkand, and Bukhara on the Silk Road. She was also delightful, and I was pleased to learn her son was a Chelsea football supporter. Over many years, Nadya has helped me prepare for a dozen visits to lands in the underbelly of Russia. She is more than a guide, more like a cross between a queen bee and Portia Fimbriata – the friendly fringed jumping spider or the world's most intelligent spider. Portia spiders are sometimes called 'eight-legged cats', with hunting tactics as varied as lion. Just like Nadya, the spider modifies her strategies as she learns from past events. Nadya had acquired the subtleties necessary for journeys in the 'stans'. She has an

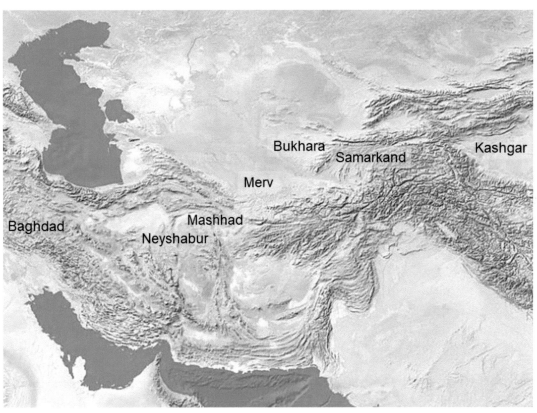

Bukhara and Samarkand to the northeast, Mashhad and Neyshabur to the southwest, with the oasis of Merv in the middle of the Karakum Desert

encyclopaedia of priceless tips as well as a vast spider's web of contacts across her central Asian region.

Nadya has another quality; she is an obsessive checker. This is very handy in the jumping spider learning process; she always made sure the freelance drivers and guides were 'on time' lest I should be let down.

Decades had passed since my last visit to the Silk Road at Mashhad in Iran. I was only eighteen then, and on my way back from India. Bukhara sits on the other side of the Karakum Desert from Mashhad. The camel caravans used to take twenty-five to thirty days to reach Mashhad from Bukhara with the giant oasis of Merv between them. I remembered, in Iran, the great trains of Bactrians with their distinctive double humps topped by dark haired tufts looking about to sprout.

Bukhara is charming and bewitching. Nadya knew all the legends as she introduced the fine mosques, squares, and of course the bazaars. My attention was immediately captivated by a silk carpet. We passed by the seller twice each day to seek an acceptable price. The silk played tricks on our eyes. From one direction the carpet was desert sandy beige, but from a different angle she changed to the colours of a rich green oasis. This couldn't be the same carpet, but she was. I knew the seller saw he had me hooked like a thirty pound trout on a five pound line, but we both enjoyed the lively banter with tea and sweetmeats.

As the afternoon cooled and a gentle breeze returned before our evening meal, I asked Nadya about her ancestry. More specifically, how had she come by her blonde hair and blue eyes?

"My great-grandmother was from Germany," she said. "My great-grandfather bought her." I wondered if I had heard correctly, but Nadya nodded.

"Gretchen was born in 1905, in Simmelsdorf, that's twenty kilometres from Nuremburg. She had blonde hair and blue eyes. Her father, my great-great-grandfather, was a merchant trading between Germany and Azerbaijan." I asked what the merchant was trading, but Nadya didn't know. Instead, she continued, "In 1918, he took Gretchen with him on a trip. She was thirteen then. On the way from Istanbul to Azerbaijan, they were both kidnapped and then sold in the slave market of Neyshabur in Iran."

Goose pimples sprouted all over my arms; how fate throws the dice with our teenage lives. I imagined young Gretchen's terror on such a forced journey east. I remembered passing through Neyshabur on my way from Mashhad to Istanbul as a teenager. That's quite a distance, over three thousand kilometres. Nadya hadn't a concern for how this came about. What mattered was that this was the girl who became her great-grandmother. She was as keen to continue as I was to listen.

"My great-grandfather Ali was from Neyshabur." I wondered about his profession and Nadya explained. "Ali was a wealthy landowner. He found Gretchen and her father in the slave market in 1918, and bought both of them. But, soon after, Gretchen's father became ill and died. Ali decided to take Gretchen as his third wife; he changed her name to Miriam."

I was curious about the other wives as well as the young teenage bride.

"Ali's first wife, Aliya, was Iranian and bore him three sons. Ali's second wife was an Azeri woman, but the marriage was childless. Miriam became pregnant soon after, and had a son, Bayram, in the spring of 1920." Just to make sure that I was not losing track; I confirmed that Bayram was Nadya's grandfather.

That evening my mind was filled with Bukhara's exquisite sights, the irresistible silk carpet, and Nadya's ancestry. I needed to ask her more. I shuddered with the thought of a thirteen year old kidnapped German girl being sold in a market. But Nadya reminded me these kinds of events are still happening all over the world. I came back to earth realising how she would see her great-grandmother's abduction differently. For her, there could not be an idea that this shouldn't have happened. Without this kidnapping, Nadya would not be here. Of course, she had a different perspective. This might be why 'history' is taught so differently in neighbouring lands. So much of the subject is perception, I mused.

At the earliest convenient moment, we continued with her family history. Of course, I enjoyed Nadya's descriptions and legends of Samanid's Mausoleum, the many mosques and madrassas. But, a personal story from these lands would help me understand much more.

Bolo-Khauz, the main Friday mosque from 1712 to 1917, Bukhara

Entrance to the madrassah of Abdulaziz-Khan in Bukhara

71

Registan Square, Samarkand. The scale is so extraordinary that the people appear to be the size of ants. A magnifying glass is helpful to see them

Nadya was eager to resume sharing her ancestry. "Ali was closely allied to Ahmad, the last Shah of the Qajar Dynasty. In 1921, when Ahmad Shah was deposed following a coup by Shah Reza-Khan, Ali had to escape Iran quickly. He could not take his whole family with him. He took his first wife, Aliya, and their three sons, together with Miriam and their son Bayram. They escaped through Azerbaijan and crossed the Caspian Sea. During their journey, Miriam had a second son, Rustam, but she died soon after."

I realised that Miriam was just sixteen when she died, leaving two sons.

"Ali brought his family eventually to Uzbekistan. They were refugees. Bayram had blue eyes, dark skin and a typical Azeri face. Ali started to produce and sell ice-cream from home, but any kind of business was forbidden by the Soviets. They were in big trouble. As non-citizens, they were told to accept Soviet citizenship and move to a village that was supposed to become an industrial town, or the family, including the children, would be imprisoned. This was how they became employed in a cement factory at Kuvasay, Fergana Valley. When he was old enough, Bayram also worked in the cement factory. That was where he met his wife, Anna. They were both young factory workers."

I asked Nadya if she could tell me about her grandmother, Anna.

"Anna's father was an Amish Siberian blacksmith, but her mother was from high society. Anna's mother had lived lavishly, owning lands in the west of the Russian Empire before the revolution, until the Bolsheviks took over and sent her family to Siberia. This was where she met her husband. But, in 1921, there was a famine in Russia. Many people, including Anna's parents, were sent south to grow food in the Fergana Valley of Uzbekistan. My grandmother, Anna, was born somewhere in Altai on their way south."

We interrupted the story to speak of the magical lands of the Altai Mountains, where Russia, China, Mongolia and Kazakhstan meet. I had long wanted to visit this region, including the world's oldest and deepest lake, Baikal, further to the east. Nadya was excited by this idea as she thought of visiting the territory of Anna's birth. We eagerly agreed to plan a trip there,

'The Ark' fortress in ancient Bukhara

The courtyard of Poi-Kalon Mosque, Bukhara

73

but haven't yet managed to go.

I was struck by a few similarities between the stories of her grandparents. Both Anna's mother and Bayram's father had been wealthy landowners, and close to the aristocracy. Suddenly, they lost everything following a change of power. Different circumstances forced them to flee during the same year, 1921, and their journeys brought them to Uzbekistan. Nadya resumed the story. "Anna was from a conservative Christian family and Bayram was a devoted Muslim. Their parents were against the marriage but, as Soviets, had to ignore religious differences. They had twin sons, Sergei and Alexander. Sergei is my father."

I thought that the family story, together with a swathe of history woven in, was complete and extraordinary. But, a few years later, I was to hear more. I was on another journey in Central Asia and came to the Fergana Valley by following the Silk Road from China. This was when I met Nadya's uncle, Alexander.

We were sitting in Alexander's house while Nadya continued the story with more details from her uncle. "In April 1986, after the explosion in Chernobyl, the authorities announced a total army mobilization. Both Sergei and Alexander had army experience, but Sergei was invited to be head of a special team to 'clean up' in Chernobyl. Sergei understood the danger of radioactivity and knew he was facing his last days with his family and especially his young children.

His twin brother Alexander, without telling anybody, went to a General in the Army and offered his candidature instead of Sergei's. He was also an engineer but unmarried. The general liked the idea and signed special papers which allowed the substitution. However, Alexander did not tell Sergei. When the day came for departure, Sergei went to the meeting point with his backpack for Chernobyl. He saw his twin brother with a backpack too and could not understand why he was there. An army man called out names from the list, and Alexander's name was called but not Sergei's, so he went home. Only much later, he discovered what had happened."

Nothing compares with the raw instincts and selfless courage of Alexander who so willingly offered himself in his twin brother's place.

The evening when Alexander and Nadya shared this part of their family story was especially moving. Sergei had recently passed away. Nadya was grieving the loss of her father and, at the same time, remembering Alexander's generosity. We spoke of how, despite the experience of working in Chernobyl, Alexander had outlived his twin. He told me the only physical suffering which remained was feeling 'easily tired' but he still enjoyed tending his vegetable garden in Fergana Valley.

At the end of the evening, Alexander fetched his Chernobyl medal to show me. He said he wanted me to have this, but I could not accept. We fought. He insisted, but I felt so strongly this was his story. The rest of his family joined in and agreed with Alexander. If he wanted me to have this medal, I would have to accept. I shall never forget that evening with him.

After writing this account, I sent my draft to Nadya for her approval. She was delighted and remembered a little more of the story.

"Alexander studied engineering in Russia at Belgorod and fell in love with a

Silk threads drying in natural red dyes, Fergana. Valley

beautiful Russian woman, Natalia. He was very romantic but indecisive. After the graduation ceremony, he wasn't able to find the courage to propose to her. He left for Uzbekistan without saying anything. After three months of missing her, his family encouraged him to go back to Belgorod, to find Natalia and marry her. He went to Russia and found her but she was already engaged to someone else. He still had a chance to change something but, instead, he wished her happiness and came home. Natalia is the greatest love of his life. Maybe this was another reason why he decided to go to Chernobyl."

Finally, Nadya mentioned that Bayram tried twice to find the gold and jewellery which his father had hidden in Iran. He would never have received permission to travel there so took illegal Gypsy routes. But he never found the place and took what he knew to his grave...

WALKING TO TAJIKISTAN

When Nadya planned my visit to the Fergana Valley, she said we would have dinner in 'a local traditional house' in Kuvasay. I hadn't twigged this house belonged to her uncle Alexander. There were many other surprises that evening; the delightful dinner with her extended family, and the moving conversation with Alexander about Chernobyl.

The following morning, my plan was to leave Uzbekistan towards the west and visit the Pamir Mountains and lakes of Tajikistan. Nadya suggested a Tajik guide she trusted, Shahboz. On the way to the border, there were two stops.

Knowing my love of bazaars, Nadya took me first to the Sunday market at Kumtepa. We enjoyed looking at their merchandise, bartering a little for fun, but mostly chatting with the people we met. For me, the market is primarily for gossip. With

my natural gregariousness, in addition to an insatiable curiosity, this chance to talk and learn is a highlight of my wanderings. The intrigue provoked others to join and the conversation became livelier.

After Kumtepa, Nadya suggested we visit Kokand, the old capital of the Kokand Khanate. We saw the Djama Mosque, Narbutabek Madrassa and the Palace of Khudayar Khan which was built by sixteen thousand slaves. These days in Fergana with Nadya helped me to connect the dots of the Mughal Emperors whose monuments in India made such an impression on me as a teenager. She explained that Babur ascended the throne of Fergana in 1494 at the age of twelve. Babur is descended from both Timur and Genghis Khan. His early rule in Fergana was troublesome, gaining control of one city only to lose another. Unsuccessful in his homeland, he left for India and defeated the Afghan Sultan of Delhi, Ibrahim Lodi, at the First Battle of Panipat in 1526 to become the founder of the Mughal Empire. I was so grateful to Nadya for her help and hospitality, together with such a rich first-hand education. History becomes alive when I see the lands and hear the stories in context.

The time had come to bid me farewell, once again, after more valuable time together. We drove to the Uzbek side of the border crossing near Konibodom, arriving at about three in the afternoon. Nadya had, as usual, planned and checked everything. As we reached the Uzbek customs; she told me she had just called Shahboz. He was waiting already on the Tajik side. I smiled, knowing her careful attention to details and for ensuring all was well.

I walked into the Uzbek customs building and found an empty hall; clearly not a busy border crossing. From previous journeys, I knew that leaving Uzbekistan is sometimes harder than coming in. They would go through everything. Over many years of travelling, I had accumulated a modest medical cabinet, knowing how far from medical facilities I might be at times. Nadya warned me that a painkiller such as codeine, for example, is illegal in Central Asia.

I knew how thoroughly the Uzbek customs would go through my photographs, check the films on my laptop, even question the book I was reading. I was prepared for that. I made sure that the last photo album I had 'visited' on my iPhone was one of nature. When the kind customs lady asked to see my photographs and I handed her my iPhone, she touched the photo icon and the phone screen was filled with flowers and trees. She said, "I see you like nature." I nodded and smiled and we looked at a few together as she flicked through. She didn't feel the need to see any more. She was interested in my philosophical book, and we spoke of that for a few minutes. I told her I didn't have any films or videos on my laptop. She looked thoroughly inside my luggage, as if she did not trust the X-ray scanner, but was happy. Soon enough, I breezed through with the required stamp on my visa and customs approval.

My new nature loving friend waved me farewell as I walked towards the wire fence which marked the edge of Uzbek territory. The ground was barren, just a few tufts of grass. At the fence, an Uzbek soldier checked that I had the exit stamp in my passport. He did not speak but simply indicated that I was free to go through the gate in the fence. I was now in no-man's-land between the Uzbeks and the Tajiks.

At first glance the ground ahead looked like a minefield. Maybe I should be careful. There were some well-trodden paths, a little muddier than the grass, so I selected one of those for the few hundred yards to the Tajik side.

As I reached the gate in the Tajik fence, a Tajik soldier stopped me. His green uniform was rather smart. He had a Kalashnikov over his shoulder but seemed a little friendlier than the Uzbek soldier I had left behind. I greeted him warmly in English but he didn't understand my words. His smile, however, suggested he understood. He replied, but in a language I didn't understand. Then he spoke again and said something in a different language. I wondered if he had first spoken in Tajik and then in Russian.

I thought he would just wave me through. Instead, he indicated that I should sit on the grass. I wondered what the delay was, but obeyed his instruction. A few minutes later, I got up. He indicated I should sit down, rather like he was gesturing to a friendly dog. This didn't make sense. I looked at him again. He did not seem malicious. There was no sign of any reason

for me to just sit there. I sat down and waited patiently. I could see a building which must be the Tajik customs but nothing was happening. Nobody was crossing the border in either direction.

After half an hour, I stood up and tried again. I attempted to explain my wish, by putting my hand on my heart, and demonstrating walking with my fingers towards the Tajik customs building. He clearly understood what I wanted. At once, he picked up his walkie-talkie and said something unintelligible before looking at me with another gesture indicating that I should sit on the ground. He was a little firmer than the last time though. More like a traffic policemen indicating a red light as he held up the palm of his right hand. At first, while he was speaking on his walkie-talkie, I had felt hopeful. The customs officials would now know I was waiting. But, why were they keeping me waiting? My perplexity increased to despair. My guard was still friendly though. Was I misunderstanding him? I wondered if he was about to come to the end of his shift. Had he just called his replacement and not customs? Would the next guard be as friendly?

I knew I needed to stay calm. But, acting like a dog on a leash was not comfortable. I continued to sit on the grass with my leash right before me, the shoulder strap holding the guard's Kalashnikov. My ordeal was clearly not going to be just a matter of a few minutes.

I regretted there were no other travellers attempting to cross this border. I could have asked them for help. There were two hours' light left. I wondered if I would still be there in the dark, or all night even. I was mad at myself for not having brought a small bottle of water and some biscuits. What was I going to do, just sit here? I wondered about returning to see the kind Uzbek customs lady who spoke a little English. But, I realised that my single entry Uzbek visa had now expired. The Uzbek soldier would bar me. Besides, the Tajik soldier hadn't indicated that I should turn back. He had only indicated that I should 'stay put'. Not rudely, not kindly, but matter of factly.

As I looked at my phone to check the time, I saw that I had sufficient mobile connection to make a call. I wondered if the Tajik guard would let me telephone someone. But, who would I call? I did not want to worry Nadya.

I wondered if the Tajik customs was already closed for the day. Maybe that was why I hadn't seen any other pedestrians in either direction. Was that why he wouldn't let me in? This possibility did not seem likely. My instincts were that, if the border was no longer open, the Tajik guard would have gestured differently. He would have found an easy way to let me know the border was closed.

I looked through my notes from Nadya and found the mobile number of the Tajik guide, Shahboz, which she had given me. I decided to call him instead. I hoped he had not given up on me and gone home after such a long delay. Calling him to ensure he was still there, and would continue to wait for me, would be wise. I wondered if the soldier would mind if I used my mobile phone; I mustn't let him think I wanted to photograph him. Tentative steps would be wise.

Still sitting on the ground, I swivelled slowly to face him and very gently gestured the idea of making a call. He didn't seem to mind. He just nodded. I called Shahboz and he answered immediately. Having introduced myself, I asked where he was.

"I arrived at the border over an hour ago and am waiting for you behind the gate just beyond the customs building," he said. I could see roughly where he meant, although I was too far away to recognise anyone. That was comforting.

I explained, "I am stuck in no-man's-land between the Uzbek and Tajik sides. I can see from here where you must be. I can see a gate after Tajik customs where a few people are waiting, but a soldier with a rifle will not allow me to walk to the customs building."

Shahboz understood and didn't seem concerned. He said he would see if he could find out what I needed to do. He asked me to call him back in fifteen minutes. I added that I seemed to be the only person trying to cross the border in either direction so he would recognise me easily. I thanked him for being there.

The next fifteen minutes were easier after speaking to Shahboz. I felt sure he would wait and help me through. I smiled at the soldier with a friendly glance, but neither of us knew what the other was thinking. What did he know that I didn't? Was the situation more serious?

After waiting and glancing repeatedly at my watch impatiently, I indicated to the solider that I would like to make another call. He nodded, so I called Shahboz back. He replied, "I have just been to the customs building and there is only one man who works there. He has gone for dinner." He paused and then continued, "We will just have to wait."

I smiled more warmly at my guard, with a happy glint in my eye now I knew. A few minutes later, the soldier's walkie-talkie came to life. He spoke to someone and then immediately gestured that I should continue to the customs building.

The solitary officer, who combined the customs and immigration roles, greeted me politely. He spoke good English. I decided not to ask whether he had a good dinner.

I was very relieved to meet Shahboz. We drove on to reach the northern Tajik city of Khujand at dusk and went immediately to the Arbob Cultural Palace. A wedding was about to begin and I wondered if we could take a look. Shahboz asked the groom's family if a foreigner would be allowed to see something of a Tajik wedding. "Certainly, and you must both sit with us at a special table," they said. As the evening continued, just like Uzbekistan, leaving was harder than coming in. They also wanted to see all my photographs from Central Asia.

At the banquet, Shahboz and I had a chance to talk to each other as well as the wedding party guests. This was the last day of August, a very busy time for mountain guides, I learned. Shahboz had been on the road every day of the month and had not seen his wife Guldasta or his infant daughter Amina for a few weeks. The wedding made him miss them more.

The morning after the wedding, we visited the Panjshanbe Bazaar. Walking through Asian markets always brings me to life; the sights, smells and tastes; the laughter and smiles, lush fruits and pretty children.

After the bazaar, we began our drive towards the mountains. Shahboz had planned for us to hike in two different mountain ranges. Firstly, we should drive to Panjikent via the Shahristan Pass and Zarafshan Valley before walking to seven beautiful lakes. Secondly, he would take me

The Arbob Cultural Palace, Khujand at dusk

The Thursday bazaar, Panjshanbe in Khujand

to the Fann Mountains and stay by Lake Iskanderkul, where we would walk. Iskanderkul is the Persian name for Alexander. Shahboz shared the local legend. Alexander and his army were camping by the lake on his way to India; his horse, Bucephalus, dived to the bottom of lake never to return again.

Soon we discovered that the Aini-Penjikent road was closed following a landslide. There was no access to the seven lakes. Shahboz was distraught. He was making frantic calls to try and rearrange our journey, by leaving for the Fann Mountains first, but this proved extremely difficult. He was tearing his hair out. Meanwhile, I occupied myself looking at maps, taking into account everything I had learned since he picked me up at the border. I asked him to pause for a second. He explained the difficulty of finding accommodation at short notice when so few had a mobile phone, and anyway the mountain region had poor signal. He was most anxious that I would be upset. But, I told him, "This is the least of your worries. I am used to challenges like this and happy to do something else. I am sure we will find easily

a plan which makes sense."

Looking at maps, the answer seemed obvious to me. But, this involved a solution he would not have thought to suggest. I decided to see if we could come to the same conclusion gently.

I asked him: "I think we should leave all your arrangements for our visit to the Fann Mountains as they are. Would you agree?" He agreed instantly, realising how difficult mobile phone communications were with the mountain regions.

"So, we just need to think of somewhere else to go for a couple of days." He agreed but could not immediately think of anywhere which would please me. Having studied the maps, I had seen that his home village, Basmanda, was just an hour and a half away. The next question surprised him.

"If you imagine that I was not with you, and you only had to take me to the Fann Mountains in two days' time, you would use this free time to go home and visit your wife and daughter, wouldn't you?" The way he responded with excitement was not a surprise. "Then, if you can find a place for me to stay, even on a floor in your village, why don't we do that? I would be very

L to R: Mother Zuleikha, Father Akram (with his grand-daughter Amina), Shahboz, wife Guldasta and sister-in-law Diffuza

Cutting apples for drying and preservation on the sunny hills

pleased to see a Tajik village." He asked if I would be willing to stay with him. "Nothing would please me more, as long as this is not a burden," I said.

We decided not to warn his family; we would just turn up and surprise them. This was going to be more fun for me than hiking around the lakes. The first planned hike was easily forgotten.

With a little extra time on our hands, we stopped at Istaravshan with her beautiful Madrassa of Abdullatif Sultan. Then we

climbed the hills to chat with families cutting up apples. Left to dry in the sun, these lasted for months. They tasted the same in winter, or so the ladies said.

A couple of hours later, after a long and bumpy track, we arrived in Basmanda. His family were so kind, and treated me royally. Two days later we set off for the Fann Mountains..

Lake Iskanderkul

Fann Mountains

*Hissar mountain
(part of the Pamir Mountain range)*

The pass, cut into the Fann Mountains

85

MERV

The story of Merv is so tragic; there is no way for us to understand the brutality of her fate. By the time King John signed the Magna Carta in 1215, Merv had grown to become possibly the largest city in the world. She had, for sure, no equal outside China. She was once the centre of everything; in the middle between Kashgar and Baghdad on the Silk Road and in the middle of the Karakum Desert. Arriving at Merv was always a delight. Weary travellers wrote about this most splendid of oases; neat streets and pretty gardens; her sweet melons and thriving bazaars, exquisite baths and unrivalled libraries to entertain them. There was even a giant 'fridge', or cold room, to chill out from the heat.

The earliest evidence shows Merv emerging from the Bronze Age around 2500 BCE. She grew so fast because of her unique location. She was to become more than a vast Karakum oasis. She was a major

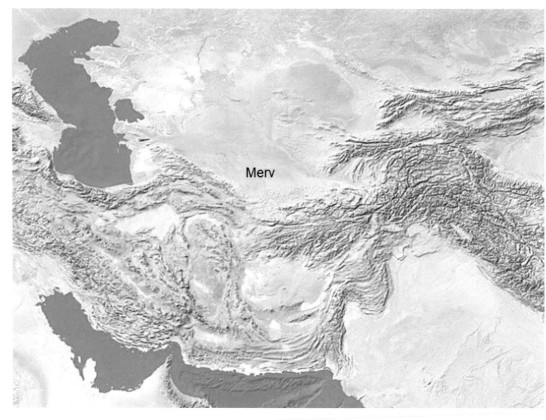

Merv

cultural centre of the world, with a civilisation to rival any of the Middle East, Egypt or Persia.

For centuries, rulers and religions came from the East or the West like winds over the desert; they mingled together. She welcomed and feasted them all. Some consider Merv as the birthplace of Zoroastrianism. She made Jews welcome. She became Buddhist with many temples and monasteries. Cyrus the Great took a fancy to her and expanded her influence in his Achaemenid Empire. Alexander the Great, an admirer of Cyrus, also came to Merv and she took Alexander's name for a while. She adopted Nestorian Christianity.

During the Sasanian Empire, from the 3rd to the 7th centuries, Merv minted their coins. She was colonised by fifty thousand Arab troops. In the 8th century a new Abbasid dynasty was declared at Merv. In the early 9th century, the Caliph chose to have his residence in Merv and she became the temporary capital of the Islamic world.

Tughril Beg came from the steppe, united the Turkmen tribes, and founded the Seljuk sultanate in 1037 at Merv. By the end of the 11th century, the Seljuk empire controlled all of the Eastern Mediterranean, including Jerusalem, lands on both sides of the Persian Gulf, and stretched through the 'stans' on the Silk Road all the way to China. Merv became the calmer eastern Seljuk capital whilst the western Seljuks were busy repelling the European knights and their crusades. As in all her previous reincarnations, she was expanded and further adorned by her rulers with the importance of her station on the Silk Road.

In the middle of the 12th century, she was known for the manufacture of crucible steel. Her life became turmoil after two centuries of Seljuk rule following the death of Sultan Sanjar. Merv entered the evening of her life with sudden and frequent changes of rule. Opposing tribes from all around possessed her successively, but could not repel the next tribe who sought to own her charms. She witnessed almost four millennia of sandstorms with competing warriors and had taken these inconveniences in her stride.

In the early 13th century, Merv was a jewel in her last empire, the Khwarazmian dynasty. This empire was not new to her; the founder, Anushtegin, was a former slave of the Seljuk sultan. Anushtegin and his successors were expanding their vassal state within the Seljuk sultanate for over a century and grew to occupy most of the former eastern Seljuk territory.

This dawning of the 13th century saw two empires wake up facing each other across a shared border. Genghis Khan's Mongol Empire to the east, and the Khwarazmian dynasty to the west, ruled by Shah Ala ad-Din Muhammad II.

Merv was at her busiest and most populous. A hundred camel caravans entered on a busy day, with some as large as 500 camels. The Arab historian, Yaqut al-Hamavi, in 1216, wrote that Merv had ten libraries richer in outstanding works than any other city. Little did he know how quickly there would be nothing left of this sumptuous Karakum oasis. Just five years later, she fell like a giant tree savagely cut down to the ground; the worst example of the butchery of a city in history.

The agony of the ground still screams so loud; all attempts to bring her to life have been blown away like shifting sands. She is a bloodstain where nothing can be crafted or resurrected.

Despite the indigestibility of her final trauma, I felt compelled to visit and sense the land of this atrocity. I knew this would not be a pleasant trip, but avoiding her was not an answer either. Having been to most of the major cities of the Silk Road, there was a conspicuous gap in the middle of the Karakum Desert between Bukhara and Mashhad, the former giant oasis called Merv.

The first step was to obtain a visa for Turkmenistan and, to my surprise, their Embassy was just around the corner in Notting Hill. I could walk there. Having obtained the necessary documents, including the downloaded visa application form and a 'letter of invitation', I visited the London Turkmen Embassy. After climbing the grand porch with half a dozen steps to a three-storey house in Holland Park Avenue, I rang the bell. A man in a suit answered and welcomed me in. He guided me to a large room with beautiful mahogany furniture. Nobody else was there. He suggested that I sit before a large empty desk. I assumed that he was a receptionist, and wondered why he wanted me to face the window while I waited. But, he then surprised me by walking around the desk and sitting down to face me. He said, "I am the consul; how can I help?"

I explained my desire to visit the ancient oasis of Merv, a missing piece of my jigsaw puzzle of the Silk Road. He smiled and asked for my documents. He checked them and said everything was in order. However, he had to follow the procedures and obtain clearance from Ashgabat. He was able to tell me exactly when my visa would be ready and asked me to come back then. Since there was nobody else there, and he did not seem rushed, I ventured a little further. I told him that I hadn't been to an embassy where there were no waiting lines, and everything was so spacious and easy.

"Welcome to Turkmenistan," he replied. He was very forthcoming. As always, I was curious; I asked him how many tourist visas per month he issued, and he told me exactly. Not very many, we agreed. He said there were a few more business visas because of the energy sector. He told me more about Turkmenistan, and where else I should visit, which was extremely kind. The meeting felt strange in only one respect. He was so friendly that I half expected him to offer me a coffee while we talked.

This felt an auspicious way to begin my adventure to the Karakum Desert. A few weeks later, I flew to Ashgabat via Istanbul with Turkish Airlines.

My first day in Turkmenistan was spent exploring the capital, Ashgabat. Here is a very modern city with smart marble buildings and only a few people in the streets. The country sits on one of the largest gas reserves but, for once, being in the centre of everything is an inconvenience. The Turkmen struggle to export their gas because they are surrounded by neighbours, including Russia and Iran, which also produce more gas than they need. The solution for Turkmenistan is to consume their energy internally and extravagantly.

There is a rumour that energy is so cheap that the people of Ashgabat leave their gas stoves burning all night to save the cost of matches. The truth, as I found out, was that the abundant wealth of energy underpins a generous state. Electricity, water and gas are provided free to all citizens, as are the first 120 litres of petrol per month with any extra costing 21 cents per litre.

Matches are indeed more expensive than gas. Perhaps they leave the gas stoves burning during the cold winter nights?

Because of the intense summer heat, and the deeply-frozen winters, the bus stops are air conditioned as was a fairground Ferris wheel. Then, the most important roads in the city have underground heating to avoid the risk of ice in winter.

I visited their Carpet Museum which boasts an impressive collection of chuvals, khurjuns and torba, as well as the two largest carpets in Central Asia. One carpet measures 193 square metres, weighs a metric tonne, and was made by forty people in 1941 as a curtain for the Bolshoi Theatre in Moscow. I wondered why this was in the museum and not in Moscow. Perhaps they made two? Subsequently, I discovered the curtain was too heavy to lift at the Bolshoi, so was returned. A wish to be biggest is not always wise.

But, I had come to see Merv. A seven-hour drive took me to Mary, a modern city twenty kilometres before the ruins of Merv and my base for three days.

The endless scrub reminded me of Afghanistan and Iran all those years ago. I had been eighteen then, and tomorrow I was visiting Merv on my sixtieth birthday. I remembered being captivated by vast caravans of Bactrian camels near Mashhad in North Eastern Iran. There is something about Bactrians; they have so much more than the extra hump. They are not only made for surviving in searing sandy heat; they are also equipped for the high altitudes and extremely bitter temperatures of the mountain passes in winter. Bactrians look regal, like lion do, whereas dromedaries look more like the more common antelope. There is also something about their darker colour and humps tufted with black hair.

Visiting Merv is eerie. The centuries of silence are palpable. My guide said that, "Unlike Bokhara and Samarkand which opened their doors to Genghis Khan when he swept through, and therefore retained some of their fineness, Merv tried to resist. She shut her doors and was destroyed after a siege." He continued, "The ruler of Samarkand was smarter. He told the people not to worry about Genghis Khan as he was a nomad and would not stay long. So they should make him welcome for a while. By contrast, the ruler of Merv had a different approach because he thought his city was much stronger."

I had also heard a different story. A few years before, Genghis Khan agreed a peace treaty with Shah Muhammad, the ruler of Merv, to improve trade between their empires. A year later, a Mongol caravan of several hundred arrived at the Khwarezmid oasis of Otrar, a hundred miles from Tashkent, to establish ties. They were massacred on the orders of the Governor, an uncle of Shah Muhammed. Genghis Khan sent three emissaries to the Shah demanding that the Governor be handed over for punishment. But the three

emissaries were executed instead. Mongol revenge was inevitable. This revenge was served by Tolui, the fourth son of Genghis Khan and the love of his life, Börte. Tolui was the butcher of Merv.

We don't know exactly how many lived there, but some say seven hundred thousand and other historians say over a million. In addition to Merv's settled population, there were so many incoming refugees and travellers that a million is very possible. In the butchery, there were just four hundred artisans spared for their useful craftsmanship. They were put to one side to be taken elsewhere. All the others were butchered.

That afternoon, in 1221, each Mongol warrior was ordered to butcher three hundred men, women or children. A million put to the sword. The scale of the slaughter is unimaginable. Some cities in history were burned, bombed, reduced to rubble by cannons or starved in a siege. But a million individual executions by sword cannot be metabolised. There sits the ground that had to drink all the blood, silenced by what happened.

Urumqi to Osh

Plans for the summer of 2015 were hatched more than a year before. Ever since my first journey to Uzbekistan, I wanted to visit the Fergana Valley. Nadya particularly wished to show me the fertile region where she grew up. Stas said he would be delighted to accompany me in the southwestern part of Kyrgyzstan near Osh, next to the Uzbek border at Fergana. Among friends, I would be able to relax whilst visiting the lushest heart of the Silk Road in contrast with the Karakum and Taklamakan deserts on either side.

The map opposite shows the Silk Road from Merv to Kashgar. The size and finery of the old cities suggest a common route across the Karakum Desert from Merv to Bukhara, continuing east to Samarkand, on to Khujand, Fergana and Osh, before climbing across the mountains to Kashgar, and then skirting north of the Taklamakan Desert. I have also included, in brown, the new highway south from Kashgar, via Tashkurgan, to Pakistan which was almost completed by 2015.

Much of what happened that summer was told at the end of the story 'Uzbek Ancestry' and in 'Walking to Tajikistan'. But, before flying to Kyrgyzstan, Martín Prechtel told me about some ancient mummies found in the Taklamakan Desert, Xinjiang, which are in the museum at Urumqi. I learned they were four millennia old, with well-preserved bodies, hair, clothing and artefacts. Some were over six-feet tall with distinctive European features including blond hair. Since my plans for Fergana Valley were already finalised, I was not keen to make a detour to China and doubted that I had enough time. On the other hand, the news of these mummies was just too extraordinary to miss, and since Urumqi is in the west of China, not far from Kashgar, I had to reconsider this possibility. I mused that I might learn something about these wandering Europeans which could help my leadership courses.

Throughout my journeys, life was made easier by attempting what appealed to me, and then being willing to accept 'fate' when something was clearly not meant to be.

I discovered there were direct flights from Istanbul to Urumqi, and Kashgar was then a short 'hop' away. I remembered, from studying maps of the different routes, that the Silk Road nearly always passed through Kashgar and I had often wondered about this westernmost Chinese city. Perhaps I would be able to cross from Kashgar into Kyrgyzstan by the Irkeshtam Pass in the 'saddle' where the Tian Shen and Pamir Mountains meet.

I emailed Kashgar Tours with a precise list of requests as there was not a lot of time to prepare. I worried that a Chinese visa could be more complicated as I only wanted to visit Xinjiang's capital at Urumqi for a couple of days before departing from an unusual border post. Not a typical 'tourist'. This might raise eyebrows in the immigration office if they wondered what I was really up to.

The next morning, Ali from Kashgar Tours replied courteously and suggested that he could manage all of my requests. Ali easily persuaded me to add two days so that he could show me more of the Uyghur culture.

Well, a few weeks later, in a taxi from Urumqi airport to downtown, I tasted a rather sharp dust like a piece of grit. With my fingers, I picked out a little black speck and realised this was coal. I remembered that Martín had said Urumqi was one of the most polluted cities on earth, and shut the taxi windows.

The next day was spent in the museum which stores the extraordinary mummies. I knew the Chinese had myths of very tall white people with blond hair, blue eyes and long noses in the western regions, and now they had found them. So the myth was true after all. Interestingly, myths usually are. Only the listeners are suspicious, but the myths are just fine. The mummies are better preserved than many of the Egyptian ones because of the extreme dryness in the Taklamakan Desert which covers most of the Tarim Basin. The 4,000-year-old mummies are from a time when the Taklamakan Desert was an inland sea, filled by rivers of melting snow from her surrounding mountains.

The photographs included here were either taken in the museum or are from an excellent guide book, 'The Ancient Corpses of Xinjiang' by Wang Binghua.

Some of the mummies were buried in a coffin shaped like a boat, reminding us that The Taklamakan used to be a sea. They had uncovered women with a red pigment on their face, buried with a red stick made from cow heart. Was this the first lipstick? The 3,800-year-old boots are in almost perfect condition.

There are different views among researchers as to the origins of these ancient mummies. The looms, weaving style, clothing and other artefacts suggest a connection with people to the west. Some of the physical features also suggest that these people could have come from the

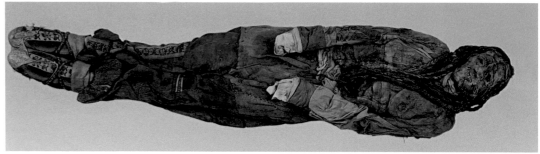

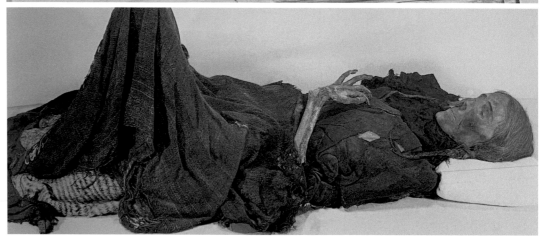

Female from tomb M5, male and female from Zaghunluq

Detail of female boots, felt books with thin silk facing and gold, painted design of hair and skin, silk sachet

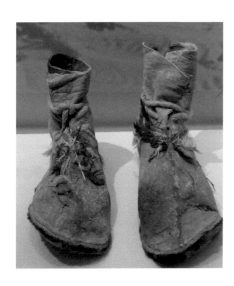

west. A few researchers went further and suggested that, "…these people must be Caucasoid Eastern Europeans who spoke an Indo-European Tocharian language and travelled east by crossing the Pamir Mountains four or five millennia ago." I wondered how they knew what language they spoke, and then learned that evidence of Tocharian languages was found a few centuries later.

Wang Binghua is more rigorous in stating the facts and seeking to avoid assumptions. I relied upon many of his pictures and writing here, although I have to confess my excitement, and a warm wish to 'own these mummies' as relatives.

Looking for some fresher air, my guide took me to the exquisite Heavenly Lake of Tianshan. The evening was spent enjoying a diverse range of Uyghur dances.

The following morning, I arrived early at Urumqi airport. I had purchased a business class seat for this short one-way flight. Occasionally, with unknown

languages and places, I feel this might be helpful in reducing the queues. The check-in desk was fast, but, at the VIP security check, my boarding pass was rejected. "The passport says Mark William Goodwin and the boarding card says markw Goodwin." They would have nothing of this. Quickly, I went back to the check-in counter. She didn't know how to solve this. The next counter changed my name in the booking and re-printed the boarding card. At security, this was likewise rejected. The manager of the check-in desks had no solution. So, I went to the information desk. The lady added 'illiam' in biro to make the w into William and then applied her rubber stamp on top. The VIP security was now happy and let me through. I felt relieved, but jinxed.

Whilst at the gate for the flight to Kashgar, my name was called out. I was taken to a minibus. All the other passengers were boarding a large bus, whereas I was alone. I asked the minibus driver if I could go with the others, but he spoke no English and waved his finger to say no quite firmly. At first, I took comfort noticing that we were following all the other passengers in their bus. But suddenly, my minibus turned the other way. I gesticulated that I wished to follow the other bus, but was ignored. I worried that I might miss the flight as my minibus was now following a baggage cart. Where was he taking me? The baggage cart was very slow.

He took me past all the other aircraft to a maintenance hangar and waited outside. By now, I was quite anxious and concerned that he was going to leave the airport altogether. There were no more planes in sight. I wondered if he was instructed to take me somewhere for interrogation. We went down a track behind some old buildings. This was not even a road. I could not see any sign of the airport anymore. He came around at a remote place at the edge of the airport, stopped, and was unwilling to continue despite my encouragement. I asked about the flight to Kashgar, but was ignored. A police and security car came, but after a few minutes they left without speaking to my driver. Then he continued to a plane around the corner. I made signs to ask if I could get off, but was told to sit down. A military guard appeared at the bottom of the steps to the plane. There was nobody else about, no sign of other passengers. Then the minibus driver indicated that I should get off the bus. Was I going to be flown somewhere else alone? They were still cleaning the plane, but a lady examined my boarding card and sat me down. Why was I alone? The hostess offered me apple juice. I realised that my mouth was completely dry. I asked the hostess why I was alone and where were we going. She said to Kashgar. "Where are all the other passengers?" Sweetly, she replied, "They will be here soon."

On the flight, I realised that all the anxiety had been entirely in my imagination. Everybody had been kind and helpful. What appeared stern or threatening to me was them simply following the rules while looking after me. The minibus driver had organised for me, as the only business class passenger, to be taken on a shortcut to the plane. During the flight, while discussing this with the hostess, I explained that I would have been happier to have travelled in the main bus with the other passengers. She explained that this was not possible. If I purchase a business class ticket, I have to follow that path.

Kashgar was a delight. Ali met me at the airport and explained his plan for me. He had packed a great deal into two days. "We will explore the rich, endless culture of the Uyghurs in Kashgar. First, we are going to the Id Kah mosque, the largest in China, and marvel at the intricate architecture of Kashgar's historic Apak Hoja tomb. We'll spend time today in the Kashgar old town and have dinner with a local Uyghur family."

"Tomorrow, we will visit the livestock market before driving up the Karakorum Highway towards Pakistan. We'll stop at Oytagh Kunlunshan with grazing animals, colourful mountains, and Karakul Lake. We will drive through the Bulungkol Valley with white sand mountains and a beautiful lake. The road crosses the Pamir plateau, the roof of the world. Karakul Lake is 3,600m above sea level and sits at the feet of the notorious, Muztagh Ata (7,546m) and Gongur (7,719m) mountains. 'Muztagh Ata' means Father of the Ice Mountain and is one the most beautiful and mysterious mountains in the world. We will visit the Stone Fort from the Han-Qing Dynasty, a Tajik village and the Tashkurgan museum." I smiled.

Tashkurgan's Tajik county was once an important hub on the old Silk Road. I asked Ali for a map. The Karakoram Highway skirts eastern Tajikistan on the way to Pakistan, through the Karakoram Mountains, and is the world's highest paved border crossing at 4,714 metres or 15,466 feet. Rather surprisingly, the border with Afghanistan is incredibly close since there is a long 'slither' of Hindu Kush, belonging to Afghanistan, which squeezes between Tajikistan and Pakistan all the way to China. The lower altitudes of the pass were still under construction and quite awkward in several places, but the trip was amazing.

Back in Kashgar, Ali showed me all the paperwork prepared for my journey over the Irkeshtam Pass. He explained there are extra complications because the Chinese immigration and customs office is at Ulugqat, more than 130 kilometres before the real border. There are a number of military checkpoints to ensure that you have the right to go to the border, and then of course they want to make sure that you don't change your mind and stay behind. I was glad that Ali's driver took me through the whole process until the last gate of

At the top of Irkeshtam Pass

China when he introduced me to a soldier. This soldier spoke English, told me to wait and then instructed a Kyrgyz truck to take me over the no-man's-land to the Kyrgyz side of the border. This did not take long, but once I saw the queue of trucks ahead of us snaking their way towards the actual customs post, I could see that around 36 hours more waiting might be needed, unless I walked… if that was allowed.

I decided to call Stas on his mobile. He answered immediately and was already waiting for me. He asked me to describe the truck, immediately got permission from the Kyrgyz border guards to drive over the no-man's-land, and found me. A few minutes later, only thirty seconds were necessary to stamp my passport before we were on our way to Osh. We had as much fun as the time when we devised the guessing game of 'K where are you?'

While re-writing this chronicle, I wondered whether there was 'news' about the people of the Tarim Basin. An article was published in 'Nature' during October 2021 based on a genome study of 13 remarkably well preserved 4,000-year-old mummies. The research suggests these earliest mummies have high levels of Ancient North Eurasian ancestry which includes cultures like the Mal'ta-Buret' of Siberia. According to Wikipedia; a boy whose remains were found near Mal'ta in the 1920s was dated as 24,000 years ago. This population is related to the genetic ancestors of Siberians, American Indians, and the Bronze Age Yamnaya and Botai people of the Eurasian steppe.

This research suggests that the Tarim mummies are indigenous people of the region, and that their physical similarities with some 'western people' could be due to both sharing some Siberian ancestry from much longer ago.

I also learned that the earliest known person with the gene for blonde hair is a woman dated around 18,000 years ago in Siberia. My family does not have anyone with blond hair and blue eyes. But, Nadya does, and so does her great-grandmother Gretchen from Germany. In Nadya's ancestry, perhaps the gene began in Irkutsk in ancient times, travelled to Europe, was brought back to Iran when Gretchen was kidnapped and sold in the slave market of Neyshabur, before becoming a gene borne by Nadya. A scientist would conclude that Nadya originated in Siberia, particularly with all the other Siberian ancestry she has, but would be puzzled as to where her European traits came from if they did not know about the kidnap of a 13-year-old.

I was pleased to learn that the Tarim mummies might still be genetic relatives, and excited to discover their indigenous home. They might not be Indo-Europeans but – to find a link with them – we just have to go much further back into pre-history. This still leaves the question: who brought the weaves and looms, artefacts and styles to our very ancient cousins in the Tarim Basin, and when? We are no wiser.

Perhaps the Silk Road was open for business much earlier than we thought.

In more 'modern times', only two millennia ago, the Loulan Kingdom is recorded as a prominent oasis in the Tarim Basin. The city was abandoned a few centuries later when the remaining lake dried up. This could explain some aspects of shared artefacts and clothing of the mummies found in the Loulan part of Tarim, but does not explain the much older ones. There must have been a Bronze Age contact between the peoples of Tarim and others from the west. Perhaps myths have clues?

This taught me how my genealogy, my clothing, my language and my culture are all separate, even though overlapping. This was helpful and became a new paradigm for later writing. But, I learned something else that year.

The summer of 2015 was clearly a time when the fates were teaching me how anxiety is manufactured by false assumptions. In the case of my departure from Urumqi, and my arrival in Tajikistan, the anxiety lasted less than an hour, or sixty minutes.

This reminds me of a family story when the anxiety lasted sixty years. My grandfather Henry had a sister called Molly. One afternoon, before the First World War began, Henry and Molly's parents invited my grandmother Eva for tea. Molly was excited to show Eva the collection of cups which Henry had won as a sprinter. But, whilst looking at them, Molly felt Eva was "…not as interested as she should have been." Molly harboured a slight grudge towards Eva and they rarely met as a result. Victorians were not experts at sharing feelings. In her later years, Eva came to live in my family house.

I remember the Christmas when Molly came over to join us all. Eva was excited to show Molly all of Henry's cups on her bedroom mantelpiece. Molly, off guard, broached the subject of that fateful tea when she first showed Eva the cups. Of course, Eva remembered the tea very well, and she was sad. She remembered her own sister Mabel was taken to hospital that morning. Mabel never recovered and died four years later. The dam burst, as Molly realised that Eva's distraction, and apparent disinterest in Henry's achievements, was fully understandable.

The difference between fear and excitement is one deep breath. Life might be filled with misunderstandings when the whole picture is unknown, and most anxieties are manufactured by imagining future events. That was my lesson from 2015.

Solitary Confinement in Burma

When I began my tour of duty in the Gilbert and Ellice Islands, I had all the required uniform for a colonial officer; white shirts; white shorts with a white leather belt; long white socks including garters like a scout, and white shoes. Approaching my leave, after two years, much was frayed. Neither the shoes nor the socks survived, but this didn't trouble me. I was happy to have 'gone native'.

In 1977, the islands were nearing independence and I had already coached my local successor, Batriti. The Government offered me a return to the Gilbert Islands after a break, but I felt this would be awkward, even if lovely. Although I could not have imagined a happier start to my career, the idea of 'a continuation in colonies' did not feel right.

I started to plan my route home, and discovered that the price of an airline ticket did not increase as long as each stopover was nearer to home. With seven weeks of paid leave and ticket flexibility, the question was where to go. I already knew from earlier conversations with my grandmother Eva that the answer would include Burma.

The local travel agency on Tarawa raised her eyebrows while digesting my requests. I think she was more used to colonial officers wanting to get home quickly. My journey began by island hopping, without any shoes, to Majuro in The Marshall Islands. Next to Pohnpei in the Caroline Islands where a young couple working for the American administration invited me to stay at their home while feasting me on lobsters. They were so kind and we enjoyed swapping our Pacific stories. After two years on an atoll with a maximum elevation of six feet, I was overawed by Pohnpei's mountains rising over two thousand feet with a jungle interior to explore. I hopped onwards to Truk, and Guam where the sight of a first traffic light since two years made me aware that I needed to buy shoes.

From Guam, I continued through the Philippines to Taiwan and Hong Kong where my cousin Rowley looked after me and shared the sad news of my Grandmother Eva's recent passing. Eva was a prominent figure in my childhood. She lived in our family home and our conversations had spawned my love of travelling.

The onward route was planned from Hong Kong, through to Thailand and Burma, before Nepal, then to India before a last stopover in Bahrein. After reconfirming all my bookings, I sent a four-word telegram to my father: ARRIVING CONCORDE EXBAH 29SEP which cost just 98 pence. I knew he would figure out that BAH was Bahrein and there was only one Concorde flight into London, Heathrow, so I could expect to be met after my long absence.

In Thailand, I loved the street markets

and the gentle pace of their lives.

I knew that Burma would be different. Unlike the openness of most of Asia, Burma was still essentially closed. Tourism had not begun. Following a military coup in 1962, General Ne Win's totalitarian rule with political violence had driven Burma into poverty. The memory of this coup remained with me since childhood. I was eight years old at the time. A fine thread of Burmese history touched my family and the connections intrigued me.

Just before the Second World War, Aung San left Burma to work for the Japanese Army to gain support for Burmese independence from Britain. He created a group of Burmese revolutionaries known as the Thirty Comrades. This group helped Japan to invade Burma in 1942. But, they soon realised their goals would not be achieved under Japanese rule; they had 'jumped out of the frying pan into the fire'. In 1944, they swapped sides, made contact with the British and helped Lord Mountbatten with the expulsion of Japanese forces. Soon after, Aung San negotiated Burmese independence from Britain and his political party won almost all the seats in the 1947 Burmese general elections.

Together with a number of colleagues, Aung San was assassinated by political rivals in July 1947 and so 'the father of Burma' did not live to see his achievements bear fruit a few months later. The first independent Burmese Prime Minister was U Nu, a close friend of Aung San; they were both activists while at Rangoon University.

Sao Hkun Hkio took a different path to becoming the Foreign Minister and Deputy Prime Minister. While Hkio was an undergraduate at Cambridge in 1934, his father was the Sawbwa, or hereditary ruler, of Mongmit, one of the Burmese Shan states for seven centuries. Hkio met his English wife, Beatrice, in Cambridge. Two years later, following his father's death, Hkio became the Sawbwa of Mongmit. Beatrice had two daughters and two sons. When Hkio's brother in law, the Sawbwa of Mongpawn, was assassinated together with Aung San, Hkio came into politics as the parliamentary representative of the Shan people. While Foreign Minister, Hkio also continued as the ruler of Mongmit.

When Burmese ethnic insurgencies began in the mid-1950s, Hkio's children moved back to the safety of Britain. His younger daughter, in her early twenties, married a British policeman and looked after her teenage brothers, Philip and David. They were our neighbours in the village of Girton, near Cambridge.

As a small boy, Burmese political violence was 'in the air' and I remember the time of the 1962 coup. Hkio was arrested and held in solitary confinement. We worried whether he would survive to see his children again.

My eldest sister, Ann, was closest to the family as Philip, Hkio's second son, used to go out with her. He was 'quite a dish' and charming whereas his elder brother David, the 'Prince of Mongmit', wore his family history more heavily. Ann describes the day, with her best friend Ingrid and my sister Jenny, they tidied up the Hkio house while David's sister was out. They washed every saucepan and piece of crockery, cleaned up after a puppy, did all the ironing, and left the kitchen and house spotless. When the sister came home, she cried. Perhaps she hadn't been so well looked after since the days when her father was the Sawbwa of Mongmit.

This memory of anxiety about Hkio's confinement and his estranged children was with me as I visited Burma in 1977. I was filled with sadness that the best of the independence leaders were 'cut down' by political opponents in 1947 or imprisoned following the 1962 coup and replaced by repressive rulers who drove Burma into the ground.

The recent loss of my grandmother reminded me of a gorgeous Burmese rice bowl she gave me. This was from Uncle Sandy who had served in the Burma police between the wars. He was shot by natives with a poisoned arrow and invalided back to Britain. Somehow our family history was meant to be touched by Burma. I wondered why history serves up so much irony. Why did the daughter of the ruler of Mongmit marry a British policeman and become our neighbour?

My days in Burma were enchanting. Despite their traumatic past difficulties with the Japanese and British, the Burmese are amongst the friendliest people I have ever met. Their delightful land will always be one of my favourites. I liked their sweet painted faces and generous smiles from their humility.

They had a charm, peace, and softness together with vulnerability. All around, the golden pagodas of Rangoon are breathtaking; such richness amongst such poverty.

Just north of Rangoon, on the way to Mandalay and Mongmit on the Irrawaddy River, I met a very beautiful woman who spoke the most exquisite English. Wondering how this came about, she said that her mother had been provided as a concubine to a British Prince and her family received a stipend from Britain for her education and support ever since. Sadly, I cannot include her photograph here.

Burma has such a mixture of Royalty and suffering, of political violence and tragedy, but her people are still generous.

KANDY PERAHERA

One of the greatest delights of my visit to Ceylon in 1972 was watching the elephants bathing at Katugastota. Especially the way they teased their mahouts. The elephant has always been my favourite animal. The calmness of her power, the grace of her movement, the essence of never having to prove her size to anyone else sets her apart. Even though there should be no other animal to fear, she still exhibits fear as if humility is one of her virtues. The delicate way she protects humans, sometimes, in ways most other animals don't. Except that she also seems to share this gift with the 'sea elephants', dolphins and whales. There are so many extraordinary similarities between her consciousness and ours. Somehow, with my deaf-sight, I knew I could speak with her and she is a great teacher.

When I left Sri Lanka, following Ceylon's change of name, I knew I would return before too long. Apart from re-visiting my oldest friend, I had to see the Kandy Perahera.

Meanwhile, I learned much more about the Perahera which only increased my excitement. Kandy's religious processions are also known as The Festival of the Tooth. The word 'Perahera' means a religious procession. Sri Lanka's oldest procession, the Esala Perahera, originally began about 2,300 years ago in the third century BCE as a series of ritual dances to pray for the annual rains. Several centuries later, when the tooth of Buddha was brought from India by Princess Hemamala and Prince Dantha, there was another procession, the Dalada Perahera. These two processions then became combined into an annual festival in Kandy, where the sacred tooth of Buddha is kept.

Together, these two festivals have given us the second largest annual procession in the world, second only to the Rio Carnival which is somewhat younger. In terms of size and antiquity, the Kandy Esala Perahera stands head and shoulders above all others. The Rio carnival procession might be longer, like the neck of a giraffe, but giraffes have nothing of the weight and power of the giant tuskers in the Kandy Esala Perahera during their ten day festival.

Nine years later, in 1981, the chance came for my return.

After passing some elephants on the way to Bahu's house, now outside Kandy in the village of Moladanda in Muruthalawa District, I found many changes.

I knew that Bahu had married, had a daughter Triloka, and I was on my way to celebrate her third birthday. But my camera slipped and distorted the candlelight. Of course, back in those days, this was not discovered until the film was developed.

There was something my oldest friend Bahu had not told me; his father-in-law was

responsible for the second elephant procession starting from Natha Devale. The surprise was even greater when I learned that his extended family also had three elephants; Raja, Rani and Podda.

On asking where they were, he replied, "In the back garden. Let's go and see."

They were more than 'just elephants'. They were also trained for the Kandy Perahera. This visit was going to be rather more than special, and the timing could not have been better.

I learned a great deal from the mahouts who look after these elephants. In India and Sri Lanka the relationship between mahouts and elephants has developed over a great many generations. The oldest evidence of captive use of Asian elephants can be found on seals of the Indus Valley civilization during the third millennium BCE. Mahouts revere the lessons received, often from their grandfathers, as this seems to be a hereditary profession. They told me: "We have to develop a very close relationship with our elephants. A milking elephant can be trained in two weeks but a mature wild elephant can take five years to train."

What they also taught was a mixture of a very warm and loving relationship together with a considerable and specific knowledge to compensate for the difference in size between the two of them. After all, the elephant may weigh seventy times more than his mahout. The mahout has a stick, with a sharp spike on the end, but this is useless against a charging or raging elephant.

The mahout needs a specialist apprenticeship and very clear communication with his elephant.

In order to protect himself, and to be able to train an elephant, he has to learn the role of seventy-two places on the elephant's body known as 'Nila'. There are three types of Nila. Some are soft places which the mahouts use "to help their elephant understand." This seems to be a euphemism for a sort of gentle smack. Then, "there are places which cause the elephant sharp pain which we use for punishment." Finally, "there are also places, where he can be killed in case of emergency." They told me an inexperienced mahout might accidentally kill an elephant while trying to control him.

On the one hand, this is clearly very cruel. The very skilled mahout never wants

to kill his elephant and does not desire to cause him severe pain. The better the communication between the mahout and his elephant, the more likely the 'domestication' can be accomplished through the training of the soft places. Perhaps this is how a young milking elephant can be domesticated in two weeks. But, how much is this affected by the awareness that his parents and elder siblings are also already domesticated? Of course, just like the way we domesticate dogs, there are rewards as well as punishments. After all, the elephant is so conscious that he needs to see some real benefits from the arrangement. Without particularities of elephant consciousness, and a strong memory, there would be no possibility to build such a detailed understanding and relationship with the mahout.

Unlike humans, who have forgotten most of their cruel domestication and are therefore susceptible to unpredictable reactions from distresses lurking in the unconscious, elephants remember everything. Elephants can remember the tricky parts, get over them, and be lovingly teasing like the bathing ones I saw at Katugastota.

One day, I asked: "What is most interesting about being a mahout?" The reply surprised me. "It is very exciting as you never know if the elephant will turn around and kill you. We are always on edge. Sometimes at night I wonder if he will kill me tomorrow. He is an animal that cannot be controlled. If you ever do anything unjust, he will always remember and punish you when you are weaker or off guard. If you use a Nila which causes him sharp pain, when you should have used a soft spot to make him uncomfortable, he will always remember that."

I learned that the Kandy Esala Perahera involves over a hundred elephants in procession. The mahouts even allowed me to help dress the elephants ready for their procession, including a giant member of Bahu's extended family.

The mahouts told me that the elephants are very conscious of the ceremony. "Their behaviour changes; the more senior their role, the more they change their behaviour. The senior elephants carrying the most important caskets will not move if one of the belts holding the casket in place on their back becomes slightly loose. They wait until

the belt is tightened and rearranged. The elephant that carries the temple of the tooth casket walks on a white cloth, like a special road. If the white cloth is not straight, or becomes furled, the elephant will stop until 'the road' is straightened out.

Only a very special elephant will accept this role. You cannot push an elephant to do so. In parts of the ceremony the elephants are in a special formation. They know exactly what to do and do not need a mahout to remind them. If the drummers stop, the elephants stop. If you put a baby elephant in the procession, she will dance to the drumbeat with all the others, but another five years are needed to train an elephant for a role in the processions."

I learned that this is clearly a very important position for an elephant, which the elephant also feels. His pride and consciousness of position is apparent. The tusker elephant, Maligawa Raja, was born in Eravur jungle in 1913 and began participating in the Kandy processions as a 24-year-old in 1937. He was promoted to the bearer of the sacred casket in 1950 and had this role for 31 years already by 1981. He continued for another seven years until he

died on 16th July 1988 at the age of 75. After having participated for fifty years, he was one of the most celebrated elephants and declared a national treasure in recognition of his service to culture in Sri Lanka, with a day of national mourning. Raja featured on a postage stamp as well as on the 1000 Rupee banknote. While writing, I wonder if Bahu's uncle designed that stamp.

I was told that Raja never had any problems with his mahouts and was very obedient to them. He always respected Buddhist priests and liked to be in the temple of the tooth. The mahouts explained that, despite Maligawa Raja's considerable qualities, we should consider his apprenticeship in the festival since 1937. No doubt the 13 years of study with other more senior elephants, before he carried the sacred casket, taught him much more than he learned from his mahouts.

Perhaps this is one of the biggest differences when compared with the domestication of an African elephant. Since elephants have a consciousness which seems to be at least the equal of ours, they need to be treated with the respect they deserve. Five thousand years are needed to build a five millennia relationship between species. Animals understand human rituals. They understand their part of the ceremony. This ritual understanding can be passed on from generation to generation in both human and other animal species.

The last procession of the ten-day festival is at night and lit by open oil torches, borne by the elephants. In years past, one of these torches sometimes fell and spilt burning oil. When elephants stepped on the burning oil, and felt a sudden fire underfoot, a stampede might rapidly ensue and people died. But Bahu told me that death was invariably caused by people who trampled on other people in the melee of the stampede. Despite their own distress, the elephants were light enough of foot to avoid crushing people. I cannot imagine another heavy animal we could give this same credit to. For such a heavy beast they are extraordinarily nimble.

After the Perahera, the mahouts also shared with me that one or two days before giving birth a mother elephant (or another matriarch) would call female relatives to create a safety area. Any males known to be potentially dangerous are chased away.

Together with many other stories from the mahouts, this experience left me in no doubt that the elephant has a great deal of consciousness, and has awareness of himself as well as of his relationship with the mahout. The ability to participate in ritual procession is special, just as the way of reordering society before a new birth, or following funeral practices.

Many years later, while writing *Mannership*, the memories of the Kandy Perahera taught me that consciousness alone is not enough to explain the uniqueness of man, if indeed there is any uniqueness. There has to be something else, particularly if we do not ignore the increase in suicide and self-harm. We might have to admit that what stands the human species apart is not consciousness, but self-harm. Some social insects may exhibit individual suicides in order to save their society. But the waste of suicide and self-harm together with self-loathing among our young without any obvious design to save the community seems uniquely human.

ANTIGUA AND GUATEMALA

A colleague of mine told me about his consulting work for a Nestlé plant in Antigua. The factory produced culinary seasonings under the Maggi brand. He said, with great conviction, how amazing this place was. Initially I was envious of his regular visits to such a beautiful island; the thought that ingredients for sauces would be sparse in the Caribbean islands did not occur to me.

Many months later, on the same assignment, he was about to travel to Guatemala. I was confused. Was he going via Guatemala to Antigua? This didn't make logistical sense. Something was odd. To my surprise, the answer was quite different. Sometimes my mind can contain such a clear picture that reality is completely missed. He was visiting a factory in Antigua, which is a very fine old city in Guatemala. I felt so foolish. Reading more about *this* Antigua, I learned that she was the capital in the 16th century and was full of tiny streets and sweet courtyards with beautiful gardens. I could not wait to pop down there and look for myself. Since I was based in Atlanta, this was an easy trip to organise.

I found a boutique hotel, Posada Del Angel, where Bill and Hillary Clinton stayed. On arrival, I thought that I had made a mistake. There was just a simple door in the middle of a long wall. A minute later, when opened, I saw a diamond among stones; such a sweet oasis of a hotel.

Before exploring the area in more detail, I learned of an opportunity to climb an active volcano, if I could get up early the following morning. Why not? I met my guide at a petrol station and he drove me to the beginning of a long walk. He said that we would be climbing to 8,000 feet. That was a lot more than I expected. At the same moment, I was approached by another man with a horse. Would I like a ride? How much? $8

On the one hand, this seemed very tempting, but I was not sure. The ground was uneven. I decided on a compromise and accepted his offer to pay $4 if the horse accompanied me, and the other $4 if I rode. This felt like a wise insurance, mindful of my suffering at altitude and exhaustion in Tibet some years before.

On a regular basis, the owner kept inviting – or should I say imploring – me to ride. But I replied, "No, I'm fine", in that voice one of my sisters uses when she isn't fine but says so anyway. After a long climb, and seeing the top a few hundred metres away, I decided to ride a little because the ground was level. I felt guilty for economising the $4. I should show my appreciation to a horse who would otherwise have climbed for nothing, and perhaps feel unwanted. I knew how

sensitive horses can be. Quite quickly, I realised that walking on my own feet felt much safer. I got off, and thanked the horse for the trial. I told him how he reassured me by walking by my side.

I climbed to the top, eventually, and felt like 'King of the Castle' as we used to say as children after climbing a mound a few feet high. Not wishing to waste a free oven, the guide toasted marshmallows. I remember being allowed, as a small boy, the same treat by the fire with a long fork at Christmas.

I loved the firm stick, a proper staff, which aided the last steps while the insurance horse waited. The owner of my horse, having received the full $8 was larking about. I told him to watch out – the horse was about to piss.

The mist to the right in the photo, near the top, is steam from the volcano. The marshmallow had a certain 'je ne sais quoi' flavour with the sulphur coating. I felt I was 'King of the Black Ash' as opposed to a simple castle.

On the way back down, I tried riding the horse again. But this was almost impossible. The downward slope was so steep that I had

Some bus rides are so pretty, the churches a delight, and the town's roofs enticing.

to lean backwards with my legs stretched out and the stirrups level with the horse's mouth, just to stop me sliding off the saddle and right over his head. No wonder there was not much demand for a horse. The idea of riding a horse up or down the side of a volcano was madness. Soon my back hurt, and I preferred to walk again beside the friendly horse. He gave me a look as if to say he was expecting all of this.

I was relieved, instead, to be able to enjoy the beautiful courtyards and gardens of Antigua, and glad to have the exercising part of my adventure behind me.

Markets always beckon me, and I was not going to miss the most colourful native market in the Americas at Chichicastenango. This is a twice weekly market for all the Mayan villages in the highlands of Guatemala, with acres of woven cloth stretching as far as the eye can see. Even the local cemetery is colourful.

After a few more churches, my last stop was by Lake Atitlan. The chronicle sent to the family reads: "I have rediscovered my taste for the ancient pathways of native tribes. Where else I can find them… Baku? Tashkent? Yerevan?"

This visit to Antigua spawned many other wanderings. A source of fresh energy, like an urge or a wind, can be hard to pinpoint sometimes. Was I provoked by my ignorance in not having known where Antigua was? Had the memory of being a 'King of the Castle' as a small boy triggered my joy? Was I moved by visiting Lake Atitlan near where Martín Prechtel used to live in a Tzutujil Mayan village – and did this remind me of how much I owed him? Were the threads of centuries-old Mayan weavings in the market pulling me?

The answer must be all of the above, in addition to other unknowns. I prefer to remember the teaching; "We don't know where the wind comes from, or where she is going, but we feel the freshness of spirit."

While day-dreaming of visiting the 'stans' and Caucasus region, particularly Baku, Tashkent, and Yerevan; an email from Czech Airlines reminded me how many of my air-miles would expire in the next 24 months. I love the way signs can line up when I am supposed to do something.

BOLIVIAN CARNIVAL DETOURS

I knew that arriving in La Paz would give me a headache. A few years earlier, my daughter Alika and I flew to Lhasa in Tibet and wondered why everybody disembarked the plane so haltingly. After a few more steps inside the terminal, headache and dizziness slowed us down too. Our bodies were clearly not designed to jump from sea level to almost 12,000 feet in one leap. Laptops can be similar; mine froze but luckily a few days later came to life again at a lower altitude before all the memory was wiped out. Just like humans, high altitudes can be fatal for laptops.

Having learned my lesson in Lhasa, I was better prepared for Bolivia and armed with Diamox, or Acetazolamide pills. I knew that this would make me pee more but the price was cheap for the benefit of avoiding altitude sickness. The tablet for the laptop was much simpler; just do not switch on when over 10,000 feet.

La Paz and Lhasa are like ancient cultural twins, both very high, although one is a few inches higher than the other. Which one is taller depends on the part of town you are visiting. I planned a day to acclimatise with easy wandering. The main square is one of the most delightful in South America. I saw some children selling small boxes of apple juice in cartons and bought a whole box to distribute to those who looked thirsty including a street sweeper, an old lady asking for coins, and other children playing. I paused often, not for thirst, but to drink copious amounts of Coca tea as recommended by Bolivians for their high altitudes.

The zebra crossings are novel. The municipality rescues wayward souls by giving them a job to show others how to cross the road properly. The 'zebras' are very jolly and made me laugh.

Part of the city looks like the moon with thousands of years of rain moulding the clay soil into moonscapes.

The following morning a guide arrived to drive me to Lake Titicaca.

After half an hour's driving on a clear road, the scenery was interrupted by a few policemen who flagged us down. The road in the next village just ahead was blocked, they said, without explaining why. Since there was no alternative route, a detour had been set up directly through a cornfield and over the mud. Rather than ploughing on, I asked my guide to let me satisfy my curiosity. Something didn't seem to fit. The police were so calm. The blockage was therefore unlikely to be an accident and the mud of the field track had been flattened by quite a few cars and trucks passing earlier. So, we parked and walked along until we found a surprise. A full carnival was in process and the main road was needed for dancing. What luck, I thought, as we joined in admiring the passion of their commitment. The ladies wear a bowler hat which is too small and 'rides' on their hair.

I learned later that this British hat came to central South America following the 19th century building of the railways. After the creation of the Bolivian Republic, over two thirds of Bolivia's trade was with Britain. The main exports were silver, tin, cinchona bark for quinine, vicuña and alpaca wool. In the 1820s the only export routes were by mule or llama. A dream of building a railway was realised and British engineers became involved in construction. Subsequently a Bolivian company managing the railway was established on the London stock exchange in 1888. Apparently the British workers found the sun stronger than they expected and received a shipment of bowler hats from Manchester. Unfortunately these were too small and, being useless for the engineers, were given to local ladies. The Bolivian fashion of wearing hats that are 'too small' continues with their ancestral story rooted in tradition and held on by a little string.

After enjoying the music and dancing, we left the tarred road to them and returned to the muddy cornfield track for our drive to Lake Titicaca. Meanwhile, I mused about all the 'hats' that cultures continue to wear because of unknown origins. This sacrifice of the only tarmac route for dancing was a wonderful sense of priorities and filled me with delight.

Titicaca, at 12,500 feet, is the world's highest navigable lake. Although the freight crossing is now managed by 'punts' large enough to carry a truck, almost a century ago the lake acquired the 2,200 ton S.S.

Ollanta. She was built on The River Humber in Britain in 1931 and disassembled before being carried by rail up to Titicaca where she was reassembled and launched. No doubt this extraordinary achievement at high altitude caused many small hats to be thrown in the air.

There is an ancient Inca temple island in the middle of the lake. After a night in Copacabana, the markets beckoned me to visit. There is no shortage of fruit.

Beginning our journey back to La Paz, after carefully manoeuvring our vehicle onto a 'punt' to cross the lake, we discovered a stowaway. She seemed in pain, all scrunched up like a church mouse. Having delicately engaged her in conversation, we learned she was 120 years old.

She heard there was a prize for the oldest grandmother but arrived on the wrong day so had to return home.

We were delighted to give her the prize money she should have won and enjoyed her prize grin.

Before leaving the lake shore we visited Paulino Esteban. Paulino built rafts for the Norwegian explorer Thor Heyerdahl and

sailed with him in the 1970s. After my fascination with his exquisite reed work, we chatted about my Pacific canoe which was also built without nails, screws or glue – just coconut fibre lashings. Paulino gave me a small model of a raft which is sitting next to me now, beside a similarly sized model of my I-Kiribati canoe. His daughter offered us a fish soup for lunch.

Continuing towards La Paz, we discovered that the carnival was still in full swing although the road was now open. The celebrations and dancers turned their attention to a bullfight and drinking session with a makeshift ring fence of trucks organised in a circle. The bulls were tethered in an adjacent field. We had arrived just in time, and they do not kill the bulls during a fight here.

Looking for a good seat, the town mayor invited me to join him as one of the judges with a perfect view perched on top of a large truck.

The first bull roared in. Clearly the matador was somewhat the worse for wear following too much beer whereas the bull was stone cold sober. The bull caught him on the arm in the first pass. As the matador

fell, the bull gored him in his back. Abandoning his fight, he staggered over to the judges showing a wound of about an inch deep with blood all over his shirt which was torn to shreds. The judges were not very impressed but we decided to award him a blanket. They recommended he get medical attention and I nodded. Other subsequent matadors were steadier on their feet.

We changed scenes to explore the ruins of Tiwanaku. I had not known that Bolivia had such an old history with the highest city among ancient cultures.

The site was probably settled with an agricultural culture in the second millennium BCE although Tiwanaku became prominent around 100 CE.

With my hearing loss as a child being such a part of my life, I was fascinated by the holes for 'eavesdropping' carved into the walls. We tried these; by putting the human ear next to a beautifully crafted stone inner ear, a conversation in the middle of the temple can be heard from more than fifty yards away.

On the way back to La Paz, I asked, "What's down that road?" The guide replied that there was nothing really. My instincts

told me to have a look nonetheless. He looked at me as if to accept the possibility of yet more luck. We tumbled on a fete including singing, dancing and costume competitions among the children; such a lovely way to spend an afternoon.

THE BOLIVIAN YUNGAS ROAD

Back in La Paz one evening, while chatting about tropical agriculture, my guide wondered whether I would like to see a part of Bolivia at a very much lower altitude where oxygen was plenty and tropical plants thrived. I asked how much lower could we descend and he replied, "Over two thousand metres." I relished this idea and encouraged him immediately. The thought of about 7,000 feet worth of extra oxygen was appealing. I looked forward to the prospect of greater warmth, enveloping humidity, and some *real breathing*. He said we could drive down to Coroico with her coffee, citric and coca farming tomorrow.

In the morning, the guide explained that we had to climb up to 4,700 metres in order to reach a pass over the top of a mountain before descending. I was somewhat relieved to know that our small van and driver would be making all the

effort as I was not at all ready for an ascent to 15,400 feet.

On the way, the driver warned me that the road down to Coroico was dangerous. I took this in my stride. After all, I had so far felt very relaxed with his driving. But when he stopped at a roadside stall to buy a small bottle of neat alcohol I was troubled. These two ideas did not seem to be compatible. I was a little concerned but kept that to myself.

The views were beautiful as we approached the first climb. The land was almost bare and very cold. Llamas were showing that the way is to stay in line.

We stopped. Both the guide and driver descended and used the alcohol for a ritual offering to mother earth, the road, and mountains, while praying for safety to reach our destination. This felt normal and there was nothing to warn me what might be around the corner. At least I understood

why they had bought some alcohol and felt foolish for not having trusted them more.

Initially the road was good.

After a while, the driver advised that we would now have to take a turning off in the direction of the smaller pass which led down towards the valley and Coroico. Noticing the narrowness of the road, I nervously told the driver, "There is no rush you know." He laughed. Then I used another tactic, "I would like to stop often for some photographs so I prefer to drive slowly." He asked me if I would prefer to drive. I smiled, reminding him that he knew the road, the corners, and the strength of his brakes. Looking back, I can see how my anxiety was growing much faster than I realised at the time.

Sometimes, while looking ahead, I could see an outline of the road snaking down the mountainside. In the distance the road appears quite tame in the way that ski slopes can when you look at them from afar. But, suddenly they can look almost vertical when you are on them. This little 'harmless' road turned out to be something quite else, as the width is only just enough for one vehicle most of the time and, while one side

is like a vertical wall of rock, the other side drops down precipitously for a very long way, thousands of feet actually.

Occasionally the road is wide enough for two vehicles to pass each other. A vehicle coming towards us took the safer side next to the mountain as if driving on the left. This didn't seem fair. Our driver had to follow suit and take the outside part of the track near the edge. I didn't think there would be enough room but he squeaked by somehow. Once we passed, I asked why he let the other driver force him towards the edge and why he hadn't been on 'our side of the road'. He replied, "We drive on the opposite side of the road on this mountain so that the driver near the edge can look out of his window to check that his wheels do not go over the edge." The idea made sense. I only just managed to avoid heart palpitations.

We came around a corner to see a waterfall spraying the road. This next section looked extremely risky. I asked to get out "to walk this part while taking some photographs" and promised to re-join him just around the corner. Initially this felt safer as the track appeared to be so much wider

while on foot. I watched the waterfall wash our van and then noticed the cross marking the spot where a vehicle had fallen over the edge. My little walk had not reduced my anxiety at all.

The driver asked me again if I would prefer to drive. I considered this thoughtfully but decided that the potential feeling of being in control was an insufficient match for someone who knew his vehicle and the mountain. He had driven this road often. I wondered if he really trusted my driving or whether he was being generous. I was not sure whether a seat belt was really of much use but decided, on balance, that staying in my seat might be better most of the time.

The views are quite breath-taking but this is easy as my breath had already disappeared.

I asked how long the drive to Coroico would take, wondering why I hadn't asked before. "Three hours," he replied. I realised that once on this journey there is no turning back; there is nowhere to turn around. And then, I surrendered to the journey and accepted what was happening more calmly for another three hours. I was scared less

often but walked occasionally to 'take the air' or a few photos. By far the worst times were whilst passing another vehicle with our left wheels just inside the edge of the precipice. Ahead of us, two vehicles came together at a place where passing was impossible. One had to reverse to find somewhere for the other to get by. I was glad we had the extra warning to avoid having to reverse. Going backwards on this track had no appeal.

We saw a group of cyclists. At first they seemed safer as a bicycle is so much narrower; a bike rider can hug the mountain and stay further from the edge. But our driver told me that quite a few cyclists go over the edge and die. Nonchalantly, I asked how often someone died on this mountain road. The guide suggested about two hundred and fifty people a year. None of this was soothing my anxieties, and

I could see that they were not teasing me but simply facing the reality. Now I understood the necessity for the ritual blessing before we began.

After this, I became much more aware of the frequent crosses marking where a vehicle had not managed to stay on the road.

My relief grew as the vegetation became lusher during our descent, like a journey from a cold desert to a tropical rain forest. Towards the end this felt like I was back in Borneo. Some of the vegetation was from another era when humans did not exist and the plants had the planet to themselves. I decided that if one started the journey with no interest in plants, then one would be a keen botanist by the bottom just from being fixated on the safer side of the road to avoid looking down.

Lunch was excellent, a beer most welcome for all except the driver since we had the journey back to look forward to. He kindly told me that we would take a longer road back, but one which was much safer.

Upon returning to La Paz, I decided to research more about this road. But, remembering the risk to my laptop at high altitudes, I asked the hotel to use their computer to avoid pushing mine over the edge.

The reading was grim. Apparently 18 cyclists went over the edge in the last ten years. The internet confirms that between two and three hundred are killed on this road every year. Unsurprisingly, most traffic is now using the much longer way around. Shortcuts are not always shorter.

Wikipedia says simply, *North Yungas road is known as 'Death Road' for all of the reasons you'd guess. Driving up or down this 43-mile (69-kilometer) switchback is extremely perilous due to fog, landslides, cascades, and cliffs that drop 2,000 feet (610 meters) at every turn.*

But my heart ached when I learned that the North Yungas Road was constructed by Paraguayan prisoners of war during the Chaco conflict. This war from 1932 to 1935 between Bolivia and Paraguay had already claimed the lives of over 100,000 soldiers and 70,000 civilians. The Bolivian Army was supported by Czechoslovakia while Paraguay was supported by Italy and Argentina. What were they all thinking? The ghosts of this road seem to be taking more every year as if one tragedy has led to a continuous flow of blood.

I was glad that I hadn't known all this in advance. But, on the other hand, I probably would not have made the journey.

ECUADOR AND GALÁPAGOS

During my tour of duty in the Gilbert and Ellice Islands, as Kiribati and Tuvalu were then known, The Foreign and Commonwealth Office wrote to me about Roger Perry. Knowing my interest in the Pacific environment, following the establishment of several nature sanctuaries, they wondered if I could find a posting for Roger. They even offered to help with a part of the cost, in case this was 'beyond my budget'. The opportunity was too good to miss. Roger was the longest serving Director of the Charles Darwin Research Centre on the Galápagos Islands.

I wrote to him and welcomed the possibility of his coming to our 'neck of the woods' to establish a reserve on Christmas Island, spelled Kiritimati in I-Kiribati. Some weeks later, Roger arrived in Tarawa and we had much to chat about. Not only about nature, but also my home town, Cambridge, where Roger received his Master's in Zoology twenty years earlier. Soon after, he set sail for the remoteness of Christmas Island; 3,300 kilometres northeast of Tarawa, and 2,000 km south of Hawaii. But, we often forget that the Pacific Ocean is a 'big place' and covers a third of the World's area.

In the years after the independence of Kiribati, I remembered fondly the work on the environment, and particularly Roger's contribution on the Galápagos and Christmas Island. The dream of visiting the Galápagos took another 35 years. By very good fortune, I met Fabrizio Prado. Fabrizio is a wonderful teacher, an exceptional guide, a 'proper' photographer, and was born on the Galápagos Islands. The wildlife photographs in this chronicle were all taken by Fabrizio.

While sailing around the Galápagos Islands, swimming behind our boat where the current was strong, I was suddenly enveloped by a fear of ghosts. The images which came to me were of all the I-Kiribati lost in the open sea, and the agony of having to decide when to give up looking for them with our limited resources. With Fabrizio's help and sitting back on deck, I reflected on how our body stores our earlier experiences, and traumas, just waiting for an unexpected trigger.

In the case of the I Kiribati, more than a few were found. They have all the world records for surviving while drifting at sea. We didn't find them, but other lands did after they drifted for months.

After sailing around the Galápagos with Fabrizio, and back on land, my interest returned to the local human species with my amateur photography.

Returning to Quito, the beautiful Basilica of the National Vow has gargoyles to remind us of Ecuador's animals, including those from the Galápagos.

The rolling hills add to Quito's charm

The evening sky has a wonderful quality. The sun's rays tease the clouds as they cross the equator with a light that entrances painters before evening bulbs illuminate the hills of Quito.

NICARAGUA

This wonderfully beautiful country seems to have everything. Two warm coasts of the Pacific and the Caribbean; Corn Islands; a giant freshwater lake called 'the sweet sea' that includes ocean specie like swordfish, tarpon, and bull sharks who visit by leaping up river; volcanoes with their own contained lakes; lotus ponds; a rich soil supporting many flowers, plants, and the lushness of her vegetation; delicious coffee; exotic Central American animals; plenty of cormorants and iguanas, and a lovely people. Delicate footprints of adults with children in the volcanic ash near Lake Managua give a glimpse of life six millennia ago.

But she has been immersed in violence in the last five centuries with a menacing regularity. Natural disasters including earthquakes, volcanic eruptions, and tsunamis have often tormented her. The name given by Julio Cortazar, *Nicaragua so violently sweet,* fits her too well.

Her treasures, and wonders, have increased her suffering. The first Spanish visitors in the 1520s were so taken by the fertility of her soil, the civilisation of her Indian tribes, and the abundance of gold that a feeding frenzy of Spanish bull sharks, or 'conquistadors' came suddenly from all directions. The native civilisation was devastated by the fighting among conquistadors who wanted everything for themselves. The Indians had neither the immunity against diseases brought from Europe, nor protection against the new weaponry. Those who survived the initial whirlwind were enslaved locally or 'exported' to Panama and further south. Adding humiliation to their subjugation, twenty Indian Chiefs were captured and set upon by ferocious Iberian Hounds in Imabite. Having dogs kill and eat their Chiefs was brutally designed to ensure submission by others.

Her indigenous name, 'Nic Anahuac', means 'us from Anahuac' and refers to the valley in Mexico where they descended from. The Spanish invaders' difficulty with pronunciation altered her name to 'Nicaragua' as if made from the Nicarao tribe and 'agua' which recalls her abundant fresh water.

The 17th century brought fresh attacks from Dutch, French and British pirates. British settlers occupied the eastern shore of Nicaragua, the Miskito coast, from the 1630s and established trade with the Miskito Indians. Although initially interested in exporting logwood and mahogany, the British encampment brought African slaves for sugar and cotton production.

Relying on an 'alliance' with Miskito Indians, the British Government thought they could split the Spanish Empire in the

Americas by invading Nicaragua. Captain Horatio Nelson, aged twenty-one, led a British naval expedition up the San Juan River in 1780 escorting an invading force of 3,000 men commanded by Captain John Polson. The anticipated support from 'allied' Miskito Indians did not arrive. Nelson's ships were able to capture the Spanish Fort following a naval bombardment, but most of the British invaders perished from tropical fevers. Only a few survivors, including Nelson, limped back to Jamaica.

This 'Fortress of the Immaculate Conception' is depicted in John Francis Rigaud's portrait of young Nelson which hangs at the Greenwich Museum in London.

In the 19th century, newly independent Nicaragua was enmeshed in civil war over which city should be the capital. Perhaps ghosts of the rivalry among the first Spanish conquistadors were awoken. Twenty years later, the British finally gave back the Miskito Coast.

This competition between conquistadors lived on in the continued conflict between the Liberal city of León and the Conservative elite of Granada. Perhaps warning us where Democrats and Republicans might be headed in the USA if they cannot find a bi-partisan ground. Once the European presence diminished,

Nicaragua was still not free. The USA stepped in to fill the gap with regular marine invasions and a 20-year occupation between 1912 and 1933.

Nicaragua had to digest American paranoia of communism once Russia and Cuba began to help her which made for a toxic battleground.

Wishing to understand this land from her different perspectives, I spent three days travelling with a guerrilla in the mountains. He won a baseball tournament in 1978 aged 14 but, on his way home, was thrown into prison accused of being a terrorist. After threats and torture, he was lucky to be let out by the initiative promulgated by Jimmy Carter. But a sense of revenge for his prison time made him the terrorist that he wasn't to start with. He went to the hills and was trained by Cuba and Russia to help overthrow the Somoza dictatorship.

While the 'terrorist' was sharing his story, we chanced upon a rural cockfight. Even Nicaraguan poultry seem enmeshed in her violent history. The cocks have weapons, razor sharp knives, taped to their legs, to inflict even bloodier wounds on their opponents. The roots of the first conquistador shark frenzy now live on through enslaved chickens.

Despite her traumatic past, the beauty of this land shines through. Her charms have enticed me to visit half a dozen times to explore more corners with a kind guide in Juan Pablo Gutierrez.

Juan Pablo is both a careful driver and a well-educated guide after his schooling in Nicaragua, Honduras and Miami, Florida. We were instantly kindred spirits seeking to understand origins of traditions that came from the indigenous culture.

Whilst reviewing this chapter, Juan Pablo reminded me that the first words we exchanged were to apologise for our respective accents. I was embarrassed by my country's colonial history and Juan Pablo was apologising for his ancestors' naïveté. He reminded me how the first Spanish to arrive were welcomed by Prince Maquil Limiski of the Nicarao tribe with a gift of 200 turkeys. The Nicarao had no fear of these new arrivals, initially.

Juan Pablo took me on tours of Managua's museums before heading to the beautiful city of Granada where the St Francis Convent is a wonderful place to learn about early history. This small museum, including artwork and Mayan statues from centuries before the Spanish conquest, generated a warm sense of Nicaraguan roots. I felt a special bond with the people of this land.

Granada is nestled on the north-western shore of the vast Lake Nicaragua. This giant lake, of over 8,000 square kilometres, contains more than four hundred islands. Juan Pablo explained that her indigenous name, Cocibolca, means a 'nest of snakes'. He suggested this might refer to the thousands of tarpon fish. Although their skin is mostly of a shiny silvery texture, the thinner ridge on the fish's back looks like the skin of an underwater snake.

Cocibolca's largest island, Ometepe, is shaped like a 20 kilometre wide dumbbell and was formed by two adjacent volcanoes with their lava forming a land-bridge in between. Petroglyphs and basalt statues confirm that Ometepe has been inhabited for more than two millennia. This culture lives on through festivals and village traditions. The trees are adorned by dark monkeys with white fur around their faces, and noisy howler monkeys sporting white fur in a more tender part of their anatomy. Returning by boat to the 'mainland', the waves in the lake give an impression that one has already found the Pacific Ocean.

Immediately, these sweet Nicaraguans reminded me of the delicious islands called Kiribati where I began my career in the Pacific. So much so, that I wondered if these two peoples were connected. Could they have migrated one way or the other? When Juan Pablo described the matriarchal nature of the indigenous Indian tribes, I was reminded that Maiana, in Kiribati, was matriarchal. Juan Pablo is an avid reader, considerable researcher, and very knowledgeable in history. Sadly, although a direct link between these two peoples was rather unlikely, the conclusion reminded us of another aspect in the common gentleness of indigenous peoples. Particularly, how they recover more easily from unspeakable traumas.

Juan Pablo's education is supplemented by earthy experiences of a family farm husbanding coffee, dairy cattle, vegetables and fruit. Together we rode horses in the mountains and coffee country, relaxed on the Pacific coast and visited the Corn Islands off the Miskito Coast in the Caribbean. We climbed a volcano before 'snowboarding' back down and riding through black dust, making me look like a chimney sweep.

León, which was once the capital, has a Museum of the Revolution as well as plenty of graffiti, ruins of early Spanish settlement, and exotic murals from her history. One evening, I became temporarily caught up in a live interview whilst attending the launch of a book of poems by a gay poet. As the only foreigner present, I was asked live on air, what I thought about a gay poet. The question seemed both shocking and extraordinary. I told them of my career which began in the Gilbert and Ellice Islands, and where there was no shame about sexuality. I returned the question to my interviewer; "Where has a culture gone wrong that Society thinks of asking this question?" Sensing that my interviewer was less liberal in his views and was interpreting my answer incorrectly, I continued, "I am proud to have gay friends who married, and gay friends who have brought up children. I am lucky to live in a culture where this can be seen naturally. Some of the North American Governments have some catching up to do. I hope your government moves in a more liberal direction."

The next morning, we drove towards San Carlos to look for a small boat to travel down the San Juan River and explore the Fortress of the Immaculate Conception where Nelson visited in 1780. Along the

way, we became becalmed in the town of Acoyapa as the road was blocked. Apparently, this was the day of the annual festival of the Patron Saint of the town and a horse parade was organised. Our plans changed instantly. The day we spent there was a delight. Many of the horses, and bulls, were ridden by young children at ease on their large animals. The town was packed, with every vantage spot already taken until suddenly a fine gentleman called us over to his house on the main street. He provided two rocking chairs on his balcony with a perfect view. His wife offered us drinks and food. We could not have wanted anything more. The memory of spontaneous generosity will always stay with me. Juan Pablo called this 'solidarity' from the indigenous tradition of looking after others.

When we finally arrived at the site of young Nelson's expedition, we had lunch alongside the San Juan River in El Castillo. The water just next to the restaurant was teeming with hundreds of jumping tarpon fish. Indeed, just like a 'nest of snakes'.

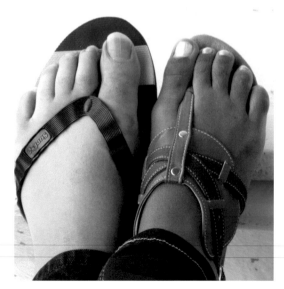

DOMINICA AND THE INDIGENOUS

I had just settled in my seat for the return flight to Atlanta after a wonderful excursion to El Salvador and was looking forward to a light lunch. Having introduced myself to the passenger on my right, I asked Trevor where he was from. "Dominica," he said. I wondered whether he might have misunderstood my reaction as he added; "Not the Dominican Republic." I smiled, and replied that there was no need to apologise for not being from Dominican Republic as Dominica was one of my favourite islands and quite different from the rest of the Caribbean. He seemed at once much happier and asked me more. I knew this was going to be an enjoyable ride together.

Luckily my iPhone contained the photographs of his island which helped to share my experience. "I like how green she is, and the magic of the rainforests that, just like a scratch on my arm after carving a way

through dense undergrowth, she grows and heals quickly overnight as if I hadn't been there."

"I enjoyed the torrent of the afternoon rains that come down like a monsoon and make some roads impassable before the sun returns quickly with warmth and intensity. I have an image of Caribbean clouds bumping into Dominica's tall peaks like an egg hitting a dry stone wall. There is nothing left of the egg, or cloud, as all the contents spill down the side of her mountains."

"I think I would wait before trying to drive over that fording pass." Trevor laughed.

"The foliage beside the roads is so vibrant with delicate flowers tucked inside." He nodded in appreciation. "The island is so friendly and open just like nature. I felt so welcome." Trevor asked whether I had a guide and, once I mentioned Agustine Macleen, his eyes lit up. We agreed how lucky I was to have such a driver from Tana Tours. He knew Tana's agency and was reassured by my choice.

The personal nature of our conversation gave me confidence to share the aspect of Dominica that moved me

Kalinago village which reminded me of the I-Kiribati maneaba

most. "But, the real attraction for me was to be able to learn more about the only island in the Caribbean that still has a Carib Indian community. I have always been fascinated by the beauty of indigenous tribes, although learning of their colonial suffering always torments me. I understood that the island was first settled by peoples from South America up to five thousand years ago."

We spoke of the Kalinago people living on the island they called 'Wai'tu kubuli' which means 'tall is her body', until

Christopher Columbus renamed her one Sunday afternoon in 1493. Although the Kalinago, or Carib people, were initially thought to have invaded this island belonging to the Igneri, more recent research and linguistic analysis has shown that the Kalinago came as a smaller group and assimilated while adopting the Igneri language, which is Arawakan from South America. Thus the Igneri culture lives on with the addition of other American traditions.

Agustine Macleen told me of the Kalinago resistance against Spanish and other colonists during several centuries. They had the advantage of a natural fortress with mountains dropping directly into the sea on one side and a lush rainforest interior. Mother Nature constantly repaired the jungle after colonial incursions with machetes and defended them well. As a result of the Kalinago defiance, the Spanish were never really able to settle in Dominica.

The first European settlers arrived when the French took control of Dominica in the late 17th century and immediately imported West African slaves to develop coffee. The French had already conquered

Dominica's neighbours to the north and south, Guadeloupe and Martinique, in the 1630s and almost all of their indigenous populations perished. However, the Kalinago in Dominica were clearly more than a challenge for France because, in the 1748 treaty of Aix-la-Chapelle, Dominica was temporarily *set apart as a neutral island for the sole benefit of the Caribs*.

Following the Seven Years War between France and Britain, Dominica became a British colony in 1763. I feel much shame for the British colonial history. Somehow we try to soothe our memories by focusing on the apparently easier parts. One of the first acts of the British administration was to survey a 'paltry' reservation amounting to 232 acres for the Kalinago Chief. I wondered if the Kalinago initially felt that they had achieved some safety but then quickly remembered how their fate was eerily similar to the American Indian tribes. British settlers harassed the Kalinago and sought to encroach on their lands. Like other parts of the world, many of the worst atrocities of the colonial period were acts of settlers and British companies. The British colonial administrators also appeared initially to have 'lost the deeds' of the Kalinago territory. This pattern became all too common in North America. Somehow, together with help from escaped African slaves, the Kalinago survived.

Many of the more benign British administrators were much younger. This reminds me of my colonial service in Kiribati. In the case of Dominica, Henry Bell was appointed Administrator at the age of 34 in 1898. Henry was fascinated by the Carib history and sent a long report to the British Government in 1902. As a result, the Kalinago territory was expanded fifteen-fold the following year with a proper survey and the Chief received a modest stipend.

After a pause for reflection, Trevor asked me where else I had been on his island. No, I had not managed to visit the Boiling Lake with her bubbling grey water, although I knew that Dominica had the second largest hot lake in the world after the Frying Pan Lake in New Zealand. I mused that of course a frying pan would be hotter. Trevor told me that the Waitukubuli hiking trail is the longest in the Caribbean at over a hundred miles. I regretted not having stayed longer on his island.

After spending most of the flight from El Salvador imagining ourselves on Dominica, Trevor wondered what indigenous traditions had interested me on my latest journey to El Salvador. He correctly suspected that Mayan temples were not the real reason for my visit.

I replied that my main interest was the archaeological discoveries at Joya de Cerén.

In the picture of a house on the next page, you can appreciate the depth of burial of between four and eight metres of volcanic dust and debris. This site shares so much with Pompeii in Italy. Both suffered sudden volcanic eruptions which covered the town in a mountain of dust and captured a moment frozen in time at the second of impact. Careful excavation has enabled a discovery of how the Mayans lived and exactly what they were about to eat that evening.

"There is one major difference which fascinates me. In the case of Pompeii, over a thousand bodies have been found. But, in Joya de Cerén, they have not found any. In both cases, most of the animals escaped unless they were tethered like dogs on chains in Pompeii and just one domesticated duck in Joya de Cerén. I wondered how the indigenous Mayan people survived. I suspect the answer is in the shaman's house."

"A number of artefacts suggest a lady shaman was living there. She had ceramic figurines, fragments of shells which look like offerings, beans, and deer antlers. They found obsidian and jade."

"Objects also include the skeleton of a mouse, decorated bowls, spindle whorls, a deer skull with red pigment suggesting use as a ritual mask and a large jug for serving *Chicha* – a fermented beer made from corn, manioc or cassava."

"Somehow my instincts tell me that the lady shaman protected the people and made sure they were safe. She might have been the

difference between all those who died in Pompeii and those who escaped in Joya de Cerén. The way that, in both cases, people left their evening meal and rushed away suggests an eerie similarity."

"There is another possibility. Many of those who perished in Pompeii were greedy. They might have gone back for their jewellery judging by what some seemed to be carrying."

"In a few hours, Joya de Cerén was blanketed by fine dust. Archaeologists have been able to discover that the eruption must have taken place in early evening in August or September. Detective work shows that farming tools had been properly stored as if just after a return from the fields. Evening fires had been lit but sleeping mats not yet unrolled. The state of the guava, agave, cacao and manioc, among other fruiting plants, together with the stores of beans suggests the exact season of the eruption."

"Perhaps, with the loss of the shamanic traditions in Pompeii, many paid the ultimate price. A shaman would have provided an 'early warning system' so that there was time for all animals and inhabitants to escape, apart from one

domesticated duck. For me, this is a reminder of how much we have lost of our indigenous understanding of nature and her forces. We need the lessons of these traditions as much as we need the plants of the forests we are destroying."

LIFOU

I had wanted to return to the Gilbert Islands, now called Kiribati, ever since 1977. But every time a plan was launched, the logistics were an obstacle. Back then, a week was necessary just to fly from London to Tarawa. Not much had changed. She was still on the International Date Line, as far from the Greenwich Meridian as is possible. Whenever other travels took me closer, like on the Pacific Rim, somehow the detour could not be fitted in. And besides, there was no point in going that far just for a few days in Kiribati.

Suddenly, fate provided enough time and sufficient air-miles. I decided to go east, through Australia. Having extra time on my hands enabled some additional treats.

An absolute must was to plan a stopover in New Caledonia. This island had always intrigued me; she must somehow have the same relationship to Australia as Madagascar has to Africa. That is to say,

apart from being a very large and long island to the east, probably not very much. During millions of years, divergent animals and plants evolved among these pairs of neighbours. Human migration came in different epochs and by different paths.

New Caledonia would be more aptly named 'Very Old Caledonia'. She has preserved plant lineages from the Mesozoic. That's the time about 252 to 66 million years ago, when dolphins, whales and porpoises were walking on earth and had not yet decided to return to their previous ocean habitat from another hundred million years earlier. A time long before Mother Nature became troubled by humankind.

Another aspect of this island beckoned me. The most intelligent bird species on earth, the New Caledonian Crow, lives there. She is smarter than the great apes. These crows don't just use twigs to forage; they have a complete toolkit in reserve. Just like

my local plumber with a white van filled with precise tools, the New Caledonian Crow has plenty to choose from and knows just what she needs for the upcoming task. But she has to make her tools from plants, and the distinctive differences of style, from one part of the island to another, distinguish the village whence each crow comes as clearly as the branded livery on the side of a plumber's van.

I contacted the tourism office in New Caledonia. "If you want to know about birds, ask Isabelle at Caledoniabirds," they replied.

Isabelle was delighted to guide me around her island. I was even happier when she told me she also knew about plants. There are so many trees that only grow on New Caledonia. And ferns; there is the world's tallest fern, all of forty metres tall. That's a fern growing seven storeys high,

New Caledonian ferns, 40 metres tall, tower over the forest...

hovering over the forest like a natural helicopter.

Isabelle also organised two additional delights for me. I wished to stay with the indigenous Kanak tribe, and I also wondered about one of the smaller Loyalty Islands. She suggested Lifou, just a forty-minute flight to the east.

Isabelle mentioned a Lifou guide of whom she had heard. She hadn't met him; he was a sort of a friend of a friend. But, apparently he was an expert on the natural habitat of Lifou. He suggested I hire a car at the airport and drive to meet him in front of the Luecila village church. The directions emailed to me were rather specific, and odd; including a precise intersection of latitude and longitude. This seemed like a spy assignation. Not finding a church on Google maps, I tried the guide's grid reference to see what came up. The answer was a bend in the village road. Feeling adventurous, I reported to Google there must be an error in their map. Google did not offer an option to report a missing church, but I could report a missing museum or temple. I chose 'missing temple'. A few days later, Google emailed to thank

me and to confirm my local report. A temple in Luecila was duly inserted on Google maps. I felt rather proud of myself for a first online map correction. On the evening before my arrival, I tried to call the mobile of my Lifou guide to confirm, but he did not answer. Perhaps he was on a trip. The idea that all of this planning was out of sync with my true objective to visit nature did not occur to me.

On arrival in Lifou, picking up a small rental car was easy enough. The first snag was that I had no internet signal. My clever insertion of the temple on Google maps was to no avail. I had printed the detail on paper though, so was able to find the spot. There was indeed a church there, but no guide. I checked across the street. Two men were building a boat. They had no idea. A few yards up the road, a family was building a house. They knew the guide's name and suggested I wait. I watched their roof thatching for a while. When they suggested that maybe something had happened and he couldn't come, I agreed.

From my experience of many wanderings, these plan failures are usually a sign that I was supposed to be doing

something else. With a small car, I would just drive around and explore this island of twenty miles wide and thirty miles tall. The rental car's glove box contained a one page map of Lifou, which I examined closely. My attention was immediately caught by a picture of a 'sacred house' in the north where the King or Chief met. The map specified that permission to visit was required as well as respecting all the traditional customs. Tourists could not park nearby, according to the map. Unusually, all the words on the map seemed to dissuade any visits.

That sounded at once much more interesting than my plans with a missing guide. I decided to drive slowly towards this village and find out more. My energy changed. Everything around me took on greater significance; details were seen which I had missed in the previous hour.

Approaching the edge of the village, I noticed a couple having a conversation across the road. The lady was on the left and the gentleman on the right. Their conversation seemed to affect the air between them, like a giant spider's web faintly vibrating. Driving onwards would have broken the web. I stopped the car and waited. Once they finished their conversation, and walked away, I inched forward. An older man was on my right. I paused to ask permission to ask him a question. He accepted. I then asked him gently if there was any possibility of approaching the sacred house.

He said, "Of course. The King is my brother and my father was the last King. Let me come with you." I opened the passenger door and he jumped in.

...and the ferns look magnificent from underneath

171

We followed the ritual customs before entering the meeting house. Once inside, we sat together for a long conversation. I spoke of the *maneaba*, the sacred houses in Kiribati and how much I loved them, and that I was on my way back to visit islands I had missed for over forty years. He replied that I was meant to be with him today. Obviously the spirits had waylaid my original guide. He remembered the way I stopped the car for the couple to finish their conversation. He had noticed my asking his permission to ask him a question before asking the question. He said that he was the only person I could have asked in order to visit the sacred house as his brother, the chief, was away. Tears welled in his old eyes. We wept together.

One of his cousins came to tend the log fire, and enjoyed the story of our auspicious meeting. As he left, he gave me a sacred regal feather.

The chief's brother then invited me to drink cava at his home. But, while saying how much I would enjoy that, there was something I would enjoy more. He looked curious. "Since I have found the guide I was meant to find, would he be willing to come with me and to show me where to go?" His

The sacred meeting house

His brother's residence

eyes lit up. "Yes, and we will visit my relatives."

As we toured the island, everywhere we went, he was warmly greeted. The islanders were all family. After their first words of greeting, I chipped in that he now had a car and a proper English chauffeur. Everybody laughed.

The east coast of Lifou.

TANNA, VANUATU

Back in 1974, when I sought the first step of my career, Magdalen College posted a 'flyer' from the Foreign and Commonwealth Office with three vacancies for a young administrator: The Gilbert and Ellice Islands, the New Hebrides, and Hong Kong.

I was immediately drawn to the first option, and selected the New Hebrides as my 'second choice' despite being a little troubled by the idea of an Anglo-French Condominium. I thought too much time might be wasted on quibbling or jostling with the French instead of helping the local population. This worry was not misplaced.

Five years later, when the New Hebrides struggled for independence, British Forces were necessary to overrule French settlers who did not support this development. I wondered where else our forces were needed to ensure independence rather than the reverse. In 1980, the islanders were able to choose a new name, Vanuatu, meaning 'Our Land Forever'.

The end of my career was the first occasion when I had sufficient time to revisit the small atolls of Kiribati. At the same time, I knew that I should see Vanuatu along my way, 'the other place' where my career might have begun.

Arriving at Port Vila, and diving into the local markets, left no doubt that I was back in the Pacific Ocean. I recognised the beetles too.

This trip had been germinating in my mind during several years. Many weeks were necessary to reach Kiribati with all the island hops. My outward route included a first visit to New Caledonia, Vanuatu, the Solomon Islands, and the way back enabled a visit to Tonga. In addition, I decided to visit two small and special islands: Lifou and Tanna with their very different cultures.

Tanna has Mount Yasur, the most 'alive' volcano in the Pacific. This volcano has been erupting a few times an hour for over eight centuries. I was comforted by the knowledge that permission to visit must be obtained from a local shaman. He would listen to the volcano and might say, "Yes, this evening is a good time," or "Definitely not – the volcano is sending up rocks the size of buses." The difference between the volcanic eruption at Pompeii, and Joya de Cerén in El Salvador, made the last minute advice of a shaman from Tanna essential.

My hotel organised a guide to take me to the volcano. We drove over miles of surrounding ash, approached Mount Yasur, and parked. We waited for permission to visit which was followed by a dance. Then, our four-wheel-drive vehicle was allowed to climb further, along a dusty track, to a much higher parking spot on the side of the volcano. We climbed on foot to the edge of the volcano's rim. A few feet further, and we might have fallen in. I felt vertiginous looking down inside and recoiled just as Mount Yasur erupted, glowing whilst spitting up rocks and sparks.

The view, coming down again as the sun set, reminded me of the stories of Captain Cook. He was also drawn to Tanna by the red glow of her volcano in August 1774.

Mount Yasur plays a central part in a true story which changed the relationship of Tanna tribes to marriage. I cannot say too much here, or my reader will not be able to appreciate the Australian film made in 2015, and re-enacted by the Yakel tribe. This film, 'Tanna', is the story of a couple's choice to marry for love, instead of adhering to local custom, with the resulting tribal disputes.

In the next days; I explored the island and met different tribes.

In traditional villages, the girls and ladies wear a grass skirt and the boys simply wear nambas. A namba is a penis sheath, or gourd, with an accompanying tassel to protect the testicles whilst giving them air. I wondered what happened when a boy became excited, and then realised that the namba must have been measured at peak performance level.

On the one hand, this proves handy protection against thorns and other potentially damaging attacks. But I wondered if the namba also enables the chance to boast. Who knows how much of the namba is filled? Another island in Vanuatu, Malekula, has both a Big Namba tribe in the north, and a Smol Namba tribe in the centre. Having studied Pacific migrations, with supporting genetic evidence, reminded me that the men of Tanna have ancestors in Papua New Guinea where the namba began. In those traditions, a man might have a softer and smaller namba for work, and a larger firm one for festivities.

The timing of my arrival in Vanuatu was during the 2018 Football World Cup, and in the days when England still had a chance of winning. My enthusiasm was shared by the children in Tanna villages, more by some and less by others.

Speaking of football, and boasting, Tanna also has the world's largest Banyan tree, the size of a football pitch. Sadly, this is too wide for a photograph.

They like to build treehouses infinitely higher than anything I dreamed of as a boy, with a majestic bamboo staircase which shows off the giant namba arriving first.

And then, they showed me their pigs before a dance.

ARMENIAN APOSTLES

When an opportune time came to travel to the Caucasus region, I decided to visit the Republics individually so their differences might be better appreciated. I selected Armenia first.

I read that Armenia became the earliest Christian nation in the world with the message brought soon after the crucifixion by the Apostles Bartholomew and Thaddeus. By 301 CE, during the reign of King Tiridates the Great, Armenia adopted Christianity as her state religion. Studying differences between the Armenian Church, the Roman and Greek Orthodox Churches fascinated me and I looked forward to learning first-hand about another branch of early Christianity.

My preparations were otherwise not thorough. I assumed since she shared her rough latitude with Turkey and Northern Iran that the spring warmth would have arrived by the end of April. The amount of

snow on the ground when I arrived reminded me that I hadn't considered her altitude, which is somewhat higher than Britain's tallest mountain. The views of Mount Ararat, in Turkey, are spectacular even though she did not come out of her clouds that day.

After a few hours of exploration, and many gregarious conversations, I sensed something else, a strong Jewish connection. As if I could feel the same DNA with similar facial features, mannerisms, jokes and habits. I was surprised how this struck me immediately, like a smell, and was absolutely certain they must share some common ancestry. Nobody minded when I asked about these similarities, perhaps because they sensed a natural and benign curiosity, but they did not know the answer. These kinds of observations always intrigue me while using the benefit of my 'deaf-sight'. Wondering how this might have come about often leads to other discoveries. I kept digging, like a cultural detective and time traveller looking for ancient links.

The extent of the Armenian Empire in pre Christian times was explained to me. Under the rule of King Tigranes the Great (95-55 BCE), Armenia stretched southwest to include most of current day Lebanon and Syria together with their Mediterranean coastline, reached across Eastern Turkey, the northern half of Iraq, and north western Iran all the way to the Caspian Sea. Perhaps Judea was also under Armenian influence when Tigranes surrendered to the Roman general Pompey in 66 BCE. The early Armenian historian, Movses Khorenatsi, writing in the 5th century, suggests that King Tigranes brought 10,000 Jews back with him when he returned north from Judea after the Roman victory. This, and learning of many other occasions when Jewish populations arrived and settled in Armenia, satisfied my observations. I shuddered on hearing an Armenian expression: "The Jews will be persecuted first and the Armenians second."

Unsurprisingly, the earliest Christian nation has many churches and very early ones too. My guide explained more of the history while driving among a vista of bright sun, cool air and a ground still waiting for spring.

Geghard Monastery is partly carved into a rock with sacred space inside the

mountain. The name means 'Monastery of the Spear' after the legend of Apostle Thaddeus who brought the spear that wounded Jesus during the Crucifixion.

My first questions included that I did not see any images of the Crucifixion, to which my guide asked why I would want to see such a gruesome image. She had a point. For Armenians, the 'empty cross' is a symbol of rebirth and regeneration. Khachkars, or cross stones, symbolically link the human and the divine.

As my journey evolved, other subtle differences with the Roman Church became apparent. I noticed a general lack of icons, as if they were respecting the second commandment of 'not making idols'.

The church at Noravank made a deep impression on me. The front door appeared to be at ground level with a stonework 'frill' or decorative cantilever edge rising from both sides towards a window. On approach, I discovered that this 'window' in the middle of the building, one floor up, was the entrance after climbing the decorative stonework 'staircase'. The width was roughly the breadth of my hips and I climbed on hands and knees with my body close to the wall of the church. Looking down, the fall would be far enough to break some bones and therefore standing up as if climbing a ladder would not be wise. Hugging the stone felt safer. The challenge brought a sense of piety on me immediately. Arriving at the top and entering the church was quite a relief.

After some reflection and consideration, whilst watching the soft morning mist through the door, there was no other way to descend apart from

repeating the ascent backwards. I felt connected to, while maintaining respect for, the many others who had climbed the stonework 'frill' in search of spiritual progression and descended silently for many centuries before me.

The contrast with the next church could not have been greater. Armenia boasts the world's longest two-way cable car in one leap. The 'Wings of Tatev' span over 3.5 miles in one suspension across a gorge to the Tatev Monastery. The ride feels like a flight to an eagles' nest perched high on a basalt plateau.

The sign outside Tatev Church explains the name St. Poghos – Petros in honour of relics of Apostles Paul (Poghos) and Peter (Petros) found when the old church was knocked down in the 9th century to build this one with her ornate doors. The site became an important university in medieval times. Like Armenia herself, the Tatev monastic complex saw periods of grandeur interspaced by eras of plunder, rape and pillage of the sacred site.

The Armenian Apostolic Church did not participate in all the 4th and 5th century councils between the Roman and Greek Orthodox churches so maintained her independent traditions. I learned that their Bible was translated into Armenian by Mesrop Mashtots in 411 CE. Unlike many European countries where the Church retained the Bible in Latin, the Armenians made a Holy Book accessible to people for their own spiritual empowerment.

From Tatev, my guide took me to the 'Armenian Stonehenge' at Karahunj. This complex of over two hundred stones, with many having a hole drilled for stellar observations, is perhaps the world's oldest observatory. Some of the stones are three metres in height and can weigh ten tons. The site may be as early as the sixth millennium BCE with many stone tombs from the Middle Bronze Age in the region; somewhat earlier than either Stonehenge or the Egyptian pyramids.

Travelling alone has often brought me luck. The following Monday morning, in a frost and early fog, I visited the monastery of Goshavank. After circumnavigating the outside walls looking for an entrance, I came around a corner to bump into a casually dressed man by the door. We were both surprised, as if not expecting to find anybody else that early, but greeted each other warmly and naturally. He asked my name and seemed moved as he asked me to wait five minutes. I wondered why, but had a friendly feeling about his request. After a few minutes of taking in the atmosphere, he suddenly reappeared, running back in his golden and red vestments, carrying an ancient bible and silver crosses. His short white hair and trimmed white beard highlighted dark eyebrows over soft eyes with side wrinkles from years of loving looks. A large golden clasp, joining the two sides of his vestment, sat over his heart. Inviting me into his church, he began to conduct a special service, with prayers including my name. As a former deaf child, I did not need to understand Armenian to feel the strength of his blessing. Then he sang several songs, also with my name, and I felt a deep joy. He bestowed a warm glow on me which lasted all day. Driving onwards, I wondered when was the last time I might have had my own service and been so blessed; probably not since baptism.

Carrying his energy and beneficence onwards, we meandered through a few more monasteries to Lake Sevan, where a

church was built in 874 CE on the ruins of the original church of St. Harutiun established in 305 CE by Saint Gregory the Illuminator. The only other people about were a General of the Armenian army escorting two visiting Russian Generals. I was reminded of the debt the British owe to Russia for their huge sacrifices in the two World Wars, without which we might not have prevailed. Unable to express this adequately, and despite the earlier blessing in Goshavank, I instead told them that we say the two best generals in the Russian army were called January and February. Luckily, this was lost in the Armenian translation, while I regretted not having been more fulsome and generous.[4]

The experience of learning about Nadya's ancestry in Uzbekistan taught me how much of historical interpretation depends on our angle of view. She would always feel differently about her great-grandmother Gretchen sold in the Neyshabur slave market in Iran as a thirteen-year-old German girl. Whilst I shuddered, without this story Nadya would

[4] This was written long before 2022. My feelings are now more nuanced although still accepting my earlier views.

not be alive. In the same way, I wanted to learn directly from Armenians about their culture in different eras.

Following King Tigranes the Great's defeat by the Romans, Greater Armenia became divided by other surrounding empires. She was subjected to the Byzantine Empire, or Eastern Roman Empire based at Constantinople, and was subsequently under the control of Persians to the East. In the 7th century, as Islam spread throughout the region, I was curious to learn from Armenians about a small Christian nation surrounded by Islam. The answer is too complex for a short story, but there were periods of some Armenian religious autonomy between frequent 'changes of control' following incursions from Turkey to the west or Persia to the east. When I learned how Armenia had been 'given to Russia' at the end of the Russo-Persian war of 1828, my ears pricked up. I asked what that period was like for them. Their reply was one of initial relief when their 'master' was a Christian nation. In 1918, just under a century later, Armenia was able to declare independence from Russia during the chaos of the Russian Revolution. But, after a very fierce and vicious wind from Turkey, she was one of the first to want to join the Soviet Union to receive protection in 1922, according to those I learned from. After the collapse of the USSR, she found her freedom again on 23 September 1991.

The Caucuses region, which includes Armenia, Azerbaijan, and Georgia, contains one of the world's earliest civilisations, the Shulaveri-Shomu culture, from about 8,000 years ago. Excavations have found a straw-woven skirt, leather shoes and a wine-making process up to six thousand years old.

I enjoyed my wanderings in this beautiful land with friendly people. I think of them often, as the largest Armenian Church in Britain, St. Yeghiche in South Kensington, is just sixty-nine metres from my home and visible from my window.

ANCIENT AZERBAIJAN

Having decided that the three Caucasus republics merited separate journeys to avoid mixing them up in my mind, I came back to this region a year later to visit Azerbaijan. The three languages use different alphabets. Imagine a bus going to the 'Silk Road'. Just below is what might be written as the destination in each language, reminding me of my difficulties with buses in Ceylon.

Armenian   Մետաքսի ճանապարհ
Georgian   აბრეშუმის გზა
Azerbaijani İpək yolu

My first excursion was to a remote and ancient village Xınalıq (Khinalug), at 2,350 metres or 7,710 feet, just a few kilometres from the border with Dagestan. For over 5,000 years this village was isolated and developed a unique language. A track was constructed in 2006. Just above sea-level in

Quba, this cuts through mountain rock, and climbs over 50 kilometres to Khinalug. In a few places, the route reminded me of the Yungas Road in Bolivia. Passing places are awkward and, just like Bolivia, sometimes require a long reverse by one unlucky driver.

I wondered what the villagers make of all the visitors who now come by. They were charming and invited me into their house for lunch. Only a few families make up the population of 2,000 souls. The air is fresh and bracing. They rear sheep, have a magnificent honey which cures 70 diseases, and are experts with herbs. There is now a museum to record some of their history.

After a family lunch, the girls insisted that I take their photograph. They have quickly caught up with much of the world around during the eight years since the road was built. I wondered whether there were any similarities with my remote childhood in silence and a quiet life until discovering the messy noises of the culture around.

My next visit was to Kish, which is only 50km to the east, but due to the remoteness of Khinalug, required a 500km journey around the mountain plateau.

According to the legends, the Church in Kish was built in 78 CE. At the end of the 20th century, the Norwegian seafaring explorer, Thor Heyerdahl, was excavating sites on the northeast coast of the Black Sea, west of the Caucasus. He found ancient metal belt holders, rings, and armbands from 100 CE near the mouth of the Don River, which were almost identical to the Viking ones found in Sweden 800 years later. Heyerdahl concluded that the Norse God, Odin, who the Swedish sagas said came from Azer, must have come from the lands now known as Azerbaijan.

Perhaps this was a factor which persuaded the Norwegian Government to fund the restoration of the Church in Kish. While excavating, they discovered that the church was nowhere near as old as 78 CE. But, they found graves and objects under the altar dated by radiocarbon analysis to

3000 BCE. Everybody is now satisfied. Since the site was sacred for at least 5,000 years; a different church may have stood around 78 CE to have provided the continuity for the legend to smile.

Heyerdahl decided that Odin was a king living near the Black Sea before taking his followers to Sweden and becoming a God in the Norse sagas. This idea may, or may not be so. But the site of the Church at Kish has benefited from the speculation.

A few minutes south of Kish sits the town of Sheki, with her famous 18th century hotel, The Yuhari Karavansaray. A whole camel caravan could be accommodated on this branch of the Silk Road. Nearby, the Palace of the Khan of Sheki was also built in the 18th century.

The remainder of my visit to Azerbaijan was spent around Baku on the Caspian Sea coast. Baku herself has a bewitching mixture of architecture from old to new.

The history museum says that Azerbaijan sits near the routes of earliest hominids from Africa into Eurasia. Homo erectus left Africa around 1.8 million years ago and the first evidence of their presence

Above: Yuhari Karavansaray. Below: Khan of Sheki's Palace

Driving south was slow, but not because of the road

in Azerbaijan is dated around 1.5 – 1.3 million years ago. The Azikh cave was inhabited 400,000 years ago by Azikhanthrop, or 'Azyk Man' and a lower female jaw of Homo heidelbergensis was found. The cave was then inhabited by Homo neanderthalensis, 65,000 years ago.

My last stop was the Ateshgah Fire Temple with an eternal flame. The nearby mountain is constantly on fire from vast gas reserves seeping through the earth. No wonder Zoroastrianism was founded around the southern coast of the Caspian Sea, among Azerbaijan, Iran or Turkmenistan.

GEORGIA

For a dozen years, my daughter Alika used to tease me because she had been here and I hadn't. One of her very best friends, Anna, was Georgian and Alika was invited to spend a summer there as a young teenager. Anna's father, Giga Bedineishvili, is a good friend; we often watch Chelsea football matches together. Another year went by, after Azerbaijan, before we found an opportune time to visit.

Georgia is a gorgeous secret gem in the Caucasus Mountains with a Black Sea coast. Like the story 'K, where are you?' I sometimes enjoyed a game with friends and even clients on my leadership courses by asking them to guess from the photos where this was. I would start by explaining that my visit was in early April. After the first picture, one said, "This looks like Scotland, with a dewy mist that rolls over the hills and dampens the grass."

The next picture of white blossom flowers and distant mountains with snow usually took their thoughts to an Alpine view. Was this Switzerland?

The carpet shop reminded them of somewhere in the Middle East.

In the previous picture, some thought they recognised Jerusalem's walls, castles and Golden Dome. But, I shook my head gently. The city dates from the 9th century. Her name is Akhaltsikhe, which means 'new castle' but this does not help discover where she is.

Next, they were sure that this was a Christian country and wondered about South America and the Andes. But, a gentle reminder of the blossoming flowers in April suggested the Northern Hemisphere.

Some houses looked like New Orleans, and statues on a bridge together looked rather liberal. Could this be near some mountains in North America?

The enormous statue of St George and the Dragon should have given the game away.

The countryside is full of beautiful churches among rolling hills.

I could not tease any longer, and had to show them a map. The rural churches remind us of the strong links of Christianity between Georgia and Armenia. Two apostles brought the message to Armenia. But, the first person to bring Christianity to Georgia was a woman; Saint Nino from Cappadocia, around 320 CE.

The town of Sighnaghi sits perched on a small mountain, with spectacular views of the snow-capped Caucasus, and boasts one of the most extensive walls and gates surrounding the city and some of her neighbouring lands.

There is a beautiful city at Mtskheta, where the two rivers Mtkvari and Aragvi join.

Mtskheta has been inhabited since the 2nd millennium BCE, and was the capital of Georgia until the beginning of the 5th century CE. Tbilisi was considered easier to defend and thus became the new capital.

Giga enjoyed showing me his wonderful country and we were never at a loss for words. We drove to the caves at Vardzia, built in the 12th century in the reign of Georgia's first Queen, Tamar the Great. Giga explained that Queen Tamar became one of the most successful monarchs, and better than some kings. Her rule is known as the Golden Age. I reminded him that we have the same memories in Britain. Our British queens have often led Golden Ages; better than kings.

The cave complex at Vardzia is constructed like at Petra in Jordan, with rooms, stairs and even a church carved out of the mountains. Why look for stones to construct a building when the mountain has already provided a roof against all elements and offers protection above ground?

The series of buildings stretch across the Erusheti Mountain and have many levels; an enormous labyrinth like a human beehive.

Our last stop was the Sapara Monastery site, hidden in the hills.

Giga was extremely kind in showing me his homeland.

In return, I wondered if I could contribute by giving a lecture at the Free University of Tbilisi, where Giga serves as dean of the business school. We chose an appropriate subject in 'The difference between Management and Leadership' and the lecture hall was full.

The students were right on the ball. They had no fear of questioning me or challenging me. Rising to enjoy their energy, I asked: "Which activities would they consider as management and which as leadership?" We all had fun with their creative and spontaneous thoughts. When I shared my summary, we found that all their ideas fitted the duality.

Management derives from the Latin 'manus' for hand and 'agere' to act implying 'acting with the hands'. Like a farmer ploughing the land, organising the flow of water since winter, and seeking to transform nature.

Leadership has roots in ancient North European languages as someone who gives confidence to follow them. The Old English word lædan is more than a guide and implies 'faith to follow'. Leadership is like a shepherd concerned for safety of the flock whilst seeking greener pastures and co-existing with nature in the wild.

In conclusion, I suggested they might now be aware how they knew instinctively much more than they thought. Unlike management that seeks to ensure problems are tackled in a specific way, leadership is about helping the instincts to flourish so we can release our potential. All too often, we do not trust our instincts. These two different approaches need to dwell in harmony. As Pythagoras taught, a man is upright when he is equally pulled by his mind and his passion.

In the evenings, Giga and I walked with his dog, Milton, named after the economist Milton Friedman. Some weeks later, he told

me that he was carrying a taser in case he met a white tiger who wanted to eat Milton for dinner. Not sure that I heard him correctly, he said the Vera River Valley had flooded and half the animals escaped from the zoo in central Tbilisi. A hippopotamus took the opportunity to swim out, but was caught by a tranquiliser dart in Heroes' Square, and pushed back. An African penguin was found after swimming to the Red Bridge Border Crossing with Azerbaijan. Some big cats, bears, hyenas and wolves were still at large. The most menacing was a white tiger.

The tiger was later found in a silk factory after he gave his hiding spot away by mauling the security guard. I wondered if the tiger felt at home amongst the smell of silk.

Luckily, Giga's house was quite high up in Tbilisi, far from the flood of the Vera River, and animals were soon returned to the zoo. Giga slept more easily, but Milton knew he was safe all along. Animals have more access to their instincts.

NAMIBIA AND THE HIMBA TRIBE

My first experience of Africa was in 1972 while hitchhiking around Morocco, Algeria and Tunisia. I was 18 then. The following year, I crossed Africa from The Nile at Khartoum to the West Coast at Dakar, before crossing the Sahara through Mauritania. That trip was undertaken with £50 of Thomas Cook's travellers' cheques and many tricky challenges. The story is told in my original 1973 journal; 'Khartoum to El Aaiun'.

Much of my career was touched by Africa. In 1983, I was asked to manage the state owned sugar industries of Swaziland and Zambia. Subsequently, we founded a company, Booker Tate, to widen the scope of management support to other tropical agro-industries. During my years with Booker Tate until 1991, we were active in Liberia, Ghana, Nigeria, Congo, Sudan, Ethiopia, Kenya, Somalia, Swaziland, Zambia, Uganda, Tanzania and Madagascar. I loved my trips to Africa to visit these large farms, and always felt instantly more alive in the heat among African smiles. During those years, I was much too busy seeking to help food production and had little time for writing chronicles.

After Booker Tate, I was involved in global manufacturing with factories in Africa. In the later afternoon of my career, I conducted leadership workshops in Eastern and Southern Africa.

I owe a great debt to two shamans from the Dagara of West Africa, Malidoma and Subonfu Somé. They are such loving and wise teachers. Other African elders, particularly the Maasai, taught me how primitive my British education was in the domain of internal aliveness and true spontaneity – a humbling discovery.

My recent excursion to the Namibian Desert was undertaken with my daughter Alika and one of her best friends, Katie. In terms of comfort, this was the opposite end of the spectrum when compared to my Sahara crossing in 1973.

Namibia's desert is reputed to be the oldest in the world. During 80 million years, the dryness has forced animals to adapt or evolve with an ability to survive with less water. Many of the big animals of Africa are also found in Namibia; they are the same specie as the ones found in lusher vegetation but subtly different. Hence they are sometimes called 'the desert rhino' or 'the desert elephant' and so on.

Namibia also has an extraordinary Atlantic coastline. The vast sand dunes, among the highest in the world, drop precipitously into the ocean. Where there are beaches, there are millions of seals. The African Penguin is here, the same family as the one who escaped from the Tbilisi zoo and swam to Azerbaijan.

The name of the desert, 'the Namib' simply means 'a vast place' in the local

Khoekhoegowab language. Fair enough. We began our trip on the Kunene River, which forms Namibia's northern border with Angola, and stayed in the most exquisite lodge at Serra Cafema. Just getting there was exciting enough. With no formal road over the soft desert sand, we skied down a hill in a four wheel drive vehicle. That was a first. Naturally, the way back up was much further around over stonier ground, to get a grip.

My interest in indigenous tribes was the reason for starting so far north, and our first visit was to a Himba village. Only the women were 'at home' as the men were away tending livestock. The Himba are considered the last semi-nomadic people of Namibia, with cows, sometimes goats or sheep for milk, and grow maize or millet when there is sufficient water. With the benefit of an interpreter, I was able to ask the elder ladies about their culture.

Much of their life revolves around finding sufficient water, and moving accordingly. No doubt; this is why most of the Himba live near the Kunene River, on both Namibian and Angolan sides.

I was interested in the different hairstyles. An elder explained that one hairstyle signified a girl who had not yet reached puberty; another meant that she was 'spoken for' in a commitment of marriage; one style signified she was married and another that she had a child of a year or more. Sensing that I was not entirely following her descriptions, the elder called four girls by name and lined them up. The change of style and age was clear, both visually and culturally. I wondered whether, in some respects, this was similar to the way my culture's ladies display their rings. I remembered reading that engagement rings began in ancient Rome as a sign of ownership. Back to the Himba, I learned that a girl cannot easily marry inside her village, so a clear advertisement of a girl's status facilitates a meeting when a boy from another village visits.

They cover their skin and hair with 'Otjize', a paste mixed with butterfat and red ochre, to cleanse as well as protect against both the sun and the dryness. The tribe is neither matriarchal, nor patriarchal, but both

– improving their chance of survival in a harsh climate with support from both sides of the family. I noticed that they enjoyed watching my daughter Alika play with an infant boy in the village. We would have liked to have spent longer with them, but the heat sapped our strength.

In the following days, we saw much more of Namibia. Some parts of the desert receive only a couple of millimetres of rain in a year, one of the driest places on earth. But, there is a phenomenon caused by the cold Benguela Current which runs up the western coast of Southern Africa – just like her cousin the Humboldt Current running up the west coast of South America – and meets warm Namibian air. A giant fog forms over the desert and provides moisture to a diverse range of plants. Animals have adapted too; some beetles have evolved to 'drink the fog'. This fog is harmful to humans, in the sense that over a thousand ships have been sunk in fog on the 'Skeleton Coast'. The coastline's name in the local language means 'The Land God Made in Anger'.

The Namib

The lodge at Serra Cafema and the Kunene River

The Himba

Otjize, made of butterfat and red ochre, to protect against the sun

Elder lady of the village, with well protected skin

Mountain Zebra

The Skeleton Coast with fog, and ballooning over the Namib

A happy daughter, Alika on the right, and best friend Katie

ANGKOR WAT

Merv suffered three generations of anxious turmoil before the sudden brutality of her annihilation one afternoon in 1221. Just 75 years before, Merv was at her finest and enjoying the twilight of Seljuk rule. The late 1140s was an excellent time for the Seljuk Empire following their victory over the Second Crusade led by the kings of France and Germany.

Another city, seven thousand kilometres to the east, was also enjoying her finest moment at exactly the same time. In 1147, King Suryavarman-II of the Khmer Empire was savouring the construction of the most expansive religious monument in the world at Yaśodharapura, or Angkor as she is now known.

Unlike the oasis of Merv in the middle of the dry Karakum Desert, Angkor boasts tropical lushness, the Siem Reap River, and the largest freshwater lake in South East Asia.

Like Merv, Angkor also suffered a great fall. Historians assumed that Angkor's destruction was sudden and violent, but maybe something else took her slowly.

The site reverberates with a millennium of harmony between nature, stone and mankind, like a giant millefeuille, and wondering which layer will be found next.

Sometimes the trees clearly came afterwards and the stones appear to be the tree's anchors and foundation like a mound under elephant's legs.

At other times one can wonder whether a door belongs to the tree, or to the stones, or to mankind.

Sometimes a ghoulish green combination confuses the mind. Was a tree supporting the stones or strangling them? Or are the roots really snakes seeking heaven?

Occasionally the roots look as if a deity had thrown down fishing nets to draw the temple upwards.

The tree roots and branches look like an ancient form of mortar between the stones. Or are they supporting pillars?

The vastness of Angkor's 292 temples is enhanced by a jungle shrieking with

thousands of rhesus monkeys, humming and rattling with the throb of insects, and the rich song of birds. There is a vibrant lushness of giant lotus flowers, plants emerging from swamps with leaves big enough to sit on or holding another small pond in their palms.

The trees often look like giraffes in disguise. Their roots are like limbs of a languishing tiger with her claws gripping the sandstone as if to say to the temple; "You might be over a thousand years old, but I am several hundred and I am alive; I can move you at will and still grip you to protect against storms." The tiger claws have grown like an Indian guru's long fingernails creeping into every recess.

Coming around a corner, and seeing yet more limbs of a tree between stones, I was surprised to find they belonged to a guard on her lunch break. Perhaps lying in harmony with the stones and nature is a level of meditation beyond my reach. Certainly she seemed in Nirvana.

I wondered if spaghetti made of limbs, nature and stones enabled a deeper sleep.

The temple was originally dedicated to Vishnu, 'The Preserver', and now appears

218

like a Hindu deity in harmony with Buddhism, which is somewhat more relaxing than the relationships between religions in Jerusalem during the 12th century.

The carvings are exquisite and lush galleries abound like giant libraries, only missing their books.

Angkor's great fall might not have been a sudden death one afternoon in 1431 following an invasion from Ayutthaya. The National Geographic says that "The cause of the Angkor Empire's demise in the early 15th century long remained a mystery. But researchers have now shown that intense monsoon rains following a prolonged drought in the region caused widespread damage to the city's infrastructure, leading to its collapse."

After days of temple visits, there was time to explore the Siem Reap River and lake.

Back on land, I wondered if I was watching an acrobatic show as motorcycles went speeding by with six or more family members travelling together, some of them standing. I dare not show you in case the picture could be used in a future prosecution. Although, perhaps I can sneak in a younger rider – she will be old enough now.

Bhutan, Land of Hidden Treasures

In the autumn of 1973, after my arduous Sahara crossing, the most likely place to find me was in the travel section of Blackwell's bookshop in Broad Street, Oxford. A small glossy coffee-table book caught my eye. The photographs were exquisite and enchanting. This gem, *Bhutan, Land of Hidden Treasures,* written by Gansser and Olschak was irresistible. Instantly my favourite, the book spent many years next to my Isle of Lewis chess set in my sitting room. I admired the photographs often and wondered when I could visit. Looking in my bookcase just now, this book jumped out at me again.

As a teenager, in 1972, I travelled to Nepal and trekked up to Nagarkot to watch the sunrise over Sagarmatha, or Mount Everest. The mountains made a deep impression on my young mind. After the struggles of the Sahara, my heart yearned for the tranquillity of the Himalayas promised by the *Land of Hidden Treasures,* just fifty miles to the east of Nepal. But Gansser and Olschak had awoken my interest before the door opened. In 1973, Bhutan was still closed to visitors.

In the following years, even when not so far away from Bhutan, I hadn't managed to visit her. In some strange way, this dream was never far from my mind, a latent desire, but I never made a plan to go. Was I saving the best for last? Or was I waiting for fate to find the right time?

Fate was not in a rush. She waited almost forty years. Suddenly, and this word *suddenly* is one of fate's favourites, an American client asked me to conduct a leadership workshop at one of their factories in Guwahati, Northeast India. The client had a specific date in mind, 4th October 2012, just over a month away. I accepted at once. Another visit to India was long overdue and I imagined all the cricket analogies which could be added to my workshop, which Indians might love. But, I still hadn't looked at a map to find where this factory was exactly.

Guwahati is beside the Brahmaputra River, in Assam. Childhood memories of geography lessons came running back to me. The Brahmaputra had captivated me since a small boy; the river in flood could be as much as thirty-seven eye-popping kilometres wide. Philip's School Atlas had graphs of the Cherrapunji rains. They had a record annual rainfall of more than a thousand inches; more than twenty-six metres of rain. The town also boasted the record rainfall for a month, 370 inches in July. I cannot recall why the black-columned rainfall charts at the back of the atlas fascinated me, but the memory of them is as fresh as the smell of my grandfather's pipe tobacco. My father used to buy him two ounces of 'Digger Shag' for sixpence.

Savouring these memories distracted me from noticing that Guwahati is the closest Indian city to Bhutan. The border is just fifty miles north of the Brahmaputra River. My heart jumped. Was fate finally beckoning me to Bhutan? My friends told me that planning a visit to Bhutan at a few weeks' notice was quite impossible, ridiculous even. There were no foreign embassies and the only way to obtain a visa was to contact the office in their capital, Thimphu. I contacted several travel agents. They were kind and helpful, but all said the same; a visa would not be possible at such short notice. They tried to discourage me by suggesting that there was insufficient time to find a hotel, a guide or transport, let alone the visa.

These kinds of challenges seem specifically designed to spur my activity. There had to be another approach. I took a first step and discovered the only airline flying into Thimphu was Royal Bhutan Airlines, called Druk Air. I called them and asked for a ticket in the days before my workshop. Initially, they were kind but not encouraging. There were no seats on the days we checked, so I suggested another,

and another. Suddenly the assistant said they had just one spare seat. In my excitement, I reminded her that I only needed one seat. A few minutes later, she found another flight with only one free seat for my return. She said that I was very lucky to have found a seat. I told her how delighted I was and how this visit was a long held dream.

I imagined she would know her country well, and I said; "Now that I have purchased a flight, how could I find a hotel, guide and the 'impossible' visa." She was so calm, and said, "Do not worry; we can do all of that for you… leave this to us."

My anxiety intruded. "But there are only three or four weeks for you to organise?"

"There is no need to worry; we will manage everything in time," she replied.

In the next few days, Druk Air prepared my itinerary. When they sent their first suggestions, I liked the disclaimer: *"We suggest that you use your itinerary as a guide rather than a fixed schedule. Unexpected stuffs always happen in Bhutan. One of our travellers met the King of Bhutan while descending from Taktsang Monastery and stopped to have a chat with him. Another went to a museum that was unexpectedly closed as the guard was home for a nap. As Bhutan*

has just opened up to the world, do not expect the service to be the same standard as visiting a museum in London. However, they are one of the friendliest and jolly people you would ever meet. I had no hesitation in leaving all the planning in their hands, particularly since they possessed the only key to my visa.

Each time another email arrived with exciting additions to my programme, I thanked them so warmly before asking gently how my visa application was 'coming along'. Their immediate response was always the same kind reply: "Not to worry. Your visa is well underway." Reading these emails again reminds me of the contrast between Bhutanese calmness and my impatience.

Just six days before my flight, an email arrived from Druk Air. *Your visa has been approved. Good karma* ☺. *Your guide is Mr. Tshering Penjor.* I smiled, thinking how easily and calmly they achieved everything. Why had I worried?

There was another surprise two days later. The last email from Druk Air said simply: *You are lucky because you will be arriving on the first day of the Thimphu Tshechu festival and will be able to enjoy the dances.* I was

The Himalayas to the west of Bhutan, the Land of the Thunder Dragon

dumbstruck. I remembered the dance photographs from *Bhutan, Land of Hidden Treasures*. This religious festival is the highlight of the year. In my excitement to find a way into Bhutan, the timing of this festival hadn't even been on my mind. Fate had certainly chosen her time well. I realised why all those travel agencies said the timing was not possible at short notice, but fate ignores what others say is impossible.

The flight from Delhi to Bhutan revealed breath-taking views of the Himalayas poking through clouds that looked like sea-foam tickling the mountains' toes. Suddenly a green patch appeared in the clouds. I saw an airfield. My first reaction was fear. I hope we are not going there. There was a steep mountain range all around so we would have to drop like a stone to arrive; like landing a plane inside a volcano crater. The aircraft banked. I hoped there was another airfield that I hadn't seen; surely the one I saw was only for helicopters? But we banked more steeply and turned, and turned even tighter, like a corkscrew, to lose altitude on the spot. Finally an access to the runway appeared feasible. The relief was palpable when we touched down. The captain told me that only nine pilots in the world were qualified to land a plane at Thimphu. I had no doubt he was right.

I stepped off the aircraft into a crisp fresh air, in bright sunshine, greeted by the ground staff in their unique Bhutan uniform, long white cuffs, jacket and kilt. The immigration officer's smile was the warmest ever welcome to a country. After she stamped my passport, I asked if I was allowed to take photographs of the airport. She replied, "But of course. Feel welcome." I wondered where else I had experienced an airport so friendly; perhaps on a Pacific Island. Tshering Penjor was waiting for me. His delight and the warmth of his handshake made me very welcome.

Driving into Thimphu amid children walking home from school in their neat red and dark green uniforms alongside the rice was delightful. I turned to Tshering and said, "I have a really good feeling about your country, she is wonderful. How have I missed her all these years?" My enthusiasm was infectious. We both knew we were going to have a wonderful time.

Tshering described his homeland as, "the only country in the world that is actually a living museum." He is right. The dances contain many tales of morality to cleanse the mind. The audience were dressed up in all their finery to enjoy the blessings.

He explained how the remoteness of Bhutan, free of roads until 1962, enabled them to preserve their culture and style over many centuries.

Tshering drove me over the 10,000 foot Dochula Pass to Punakha, the ancient capital of Bhutan.

The air is so clear and fresh with scented pine and cedar forests. This wonderful kingdom, the only 'officially' Buddhist country, has much to teach us, particularly in the realm of happiness, as their ancient capital was so aptly named. As long ago as 1971, they realised that the 'Western economic measure' of GDP was fundamentally flawed. Instead, they sought to improve their national happiness. Tshering and I enjoyed our meandering conversations. I remembered, during many visits to Asia, the lands where I felt most at peace were the Buddhist ones.

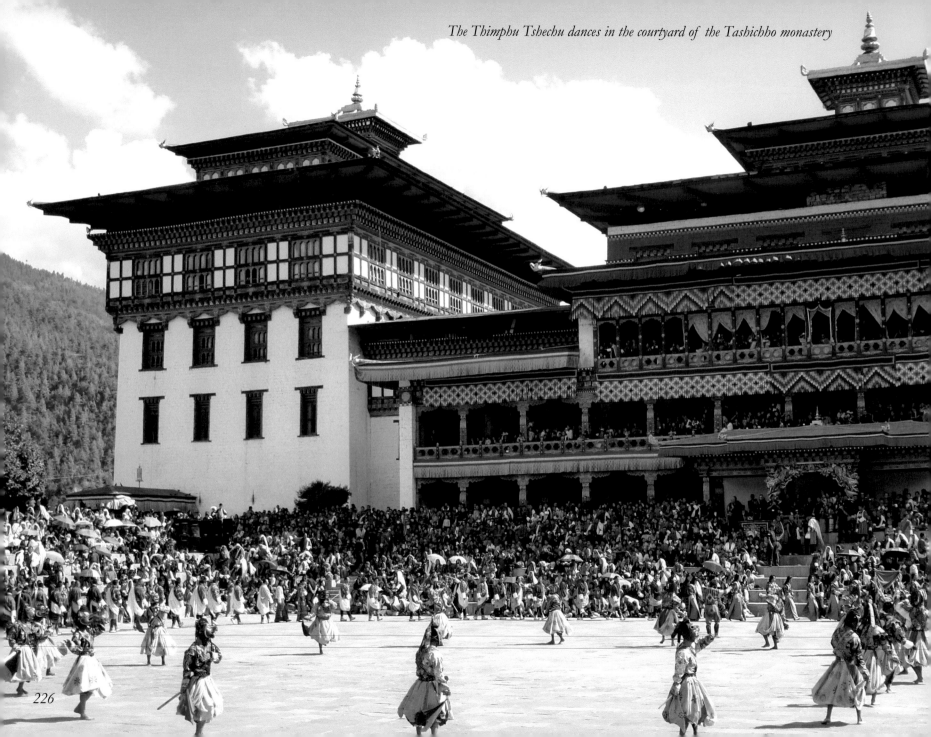

The Thimphu Tshechu dances in the courtyard of the Tashichho monastery

226

227

Thimphu Tshechu festival dances. The dance depicting the Day of Judgment lasts for five hours.

'Palace of Great Happiness' built in 1637

The Tiger's Nest, Taktsang Monastery, Bhutan, just hanging on to the cliff at 10,232 feet

After a few days together, Tshering told me that the best of my visit to Bhutan was saved for my last day. I could not imagine anything more special than we had already seen. Normally, he said he would like to surprise me, but he felt the need to warn that we would have to climb quite high and asked if I ready for this? I wondered about his sore ankle and how he would manage. When I asked where we were going, he replied, "To the Taktsang Palphug Monastery, the Tiger's Nest."

I told him that I had read about this climb and thought much of the way could be undertaken on a horse. He nodded. When I asked how much a horse cost to rent for a day, the answer was $8. That seemed a bargain. I suggested he let me rent two horses so that he could ride with me.

The following morning, we were up early and found the owner of a few horses. Our two were ready. Immediately I noticed that there were no reins. Surprised, I asked, "How do I steer?" The owner was amused by my question. "You talk to him," he said.

I realised that he was serious. I was just about to say that I don't speak Bhutanese before I paused to think. The horse would not speak English either. The owner added, while I was digesting my predicament, "The horse knows the way."

On my leadership courses, I used to explain that the horse is one of the most emotionally sensitive and attuned animals. He can smell what the rider is thinking. I used to tell them that if you ride a horse fast down a hill and attempt to jump a fence, and if you have the slightest doubt whether you can get over, then the horse will smell your doubt and back up. So, you might still go over the fence… but not with the horse. But now I was going to have to put my own teaching to the test on a narrow mountain path with a sheer edge dropping down thousands of feet. I would have to rely on the horse knowing what I was thinking or feeling.

At first this was straightforward; the path was wide and the horse knew the way. But, after a short steep climb he started to pant, breathing very fast. I feared his heart and body would explode. I reassured him, and suggested he should stop for a few minutes to cool down. He understood immediately. I was not in a rush, and very grateful for my ride. Once his temperature and level of exhaustion reduced, I suggested he could start again. He did. We had a few more stops for breath on the way. I told him he was such a fine horse and I liked him. He understood me very well. We had only one area of disagreement, however. Much higher up the mountain, the path was very narrow and the drop on my right was precipitous and sheer. I could not bear to look. I wanted the horse to stay close to the left side of the path, nearer to the rock face but he preferred the right side close to the edge. Several times I had to ask him to move left and he did. But then surreptitiously he moved again towards the right. I wondered why.

Noticing that the ground near the edge was soft mud, whereas the ground near the mountain rock face had sharper stones, I told him that now I understood. Could we walk more slowly so that he could avoid the difficult stones but still stay on the left side where the path was less scary for me? He agreed and helped me to relax, for which I was immensely grateful. I was pleased to have a new horse story variant for my workshop on leadership in Guwahati the following week.

This visit reminded me of something which James Hillman taught me. "The most beautiful moments of your life are always when you are out of control, and yet you spend most of your life trying to stay in control."

In the case of Bhutan, Hillman was spot on. Fate had been the guide for this visit, and had achieved more than I could have dreamed of. Perhaps this was why I revelled in my unexpected journey from the memory of the Cherrapungi rains and the smell of my grandfather's tobacco all the way to the Tiger's Nest. Maybe, somewhere or somehow, a part of me knew that my time to visit this special Kingdom would be decided for me.

BACK TO THE BEGINNING… FREE BENGAL

I enjoyed my workshop in Guwahati, India, on the Brahmaputra River. They liked the cricket metaphors, especially my admission that the English team was not the finest, and they roared with laughter when I shared how often I took the wrong direction in India as a teenager. They reluctantly admitted this unique Indian charm of always giving directions, irrespective of whether they knew the way.

Perhaps, I should have titled my leadership workshop 'knowing the right direction'.

A few weeks earlier, while preparing this course and thinking of India, I remembered how all my travelling began. The first trip to India was planned and saved for during two teenage years. But just as the final touches were applied, everything was thrown off course by East Pakistan's brutal struggle for autonomy. Luckily, the war lasted only 13 days until the West Pakistan

236

forces in the East surrendered to India, the 'mid-wife' of a new nation; 'the land of Bengal' or Bangladesh.

My freedom as a wanderer, and my first journey in the Indian sub-continent, was intricately bound up with the birth of Bangladesh. I decided to visit her, at long last, as soon as the Guwahati workshop concluded.

I imagined that the capital, Dhaka would be like Calcutta, and was expecting the hustle and bustle of rickshaws and fast weaving traffic.

I was not expecting such interesting new architecture, particularly their parliament building looking like a light mauve Jarlsberg cheese.

Everybody was friendly and smiling, even when in a rush, and stalls were neat.

A small boy offered to show me around and we climbed all over the river packed with boats.

I thought that the water traffic was like Istanbul on the Bosporus, except ten times as crowded.

After the teeming city, I was happy to visit the calmness of the countryside on the way to Bengal's ancient capital Sonargaon.

237

We passed lush ponds and the Goaldi Mosque with her rusty coloured walls, before arriving in almost deserted streets of the old Sonargaon, which was founded in 1281.

Once inside Sonargaon, I found a small village school with 70 boys in class, aged about ten. I walked in and greeted them all. The teacher was amused, and told me he was leading a maths class. When I asked what he was teaching, he replied "Algebra." I must have been triggered by an ancient memory of being ten years old and helping my teacher with the maths teaching. Spontaneously, I asked if he would mind if I set a test. He smiled, and said, "Why not." I wrote a few equations on the blackboard with chalk, just like fifty years before. A smart boy in the back row got them all right. I felt he was a kindred spirit as maths was always my favourite and easiest subject.

Continuing my tour of town, I savoured the fun of a stranger setting a test. I wondered what the boys made of the distraction, and hoped they developed more motivation to learn algebra.

THE JOURNEY OF A MONGOLIAN COAT

In the autumn of 2009, I was asked to deliver a lecture on leadership in Hohhot, the capital of Inner Mongolia. The requested date was in the following January. Having wanted to visit Mongolia herself for many years, I was filled with excitement at this possibility. The increase in my wanderings whilst riding on the back of client requests always felt propitious.

The first step seemed auspiciously easy as the Mongolian Embassy is just around the corner in Kensington Court, hidden on one of the smaller streets. Once I had descended the black iron stairs to the lower ground floor, the lady consul could not have been more charming. She even had the time to suggest where to visit, who to ask as a guide, and recommended hotels. Everything seemed very straightforward.

Perhaps the demand for visas is lower in mid-winter. As I stood up to leave, she warned me that the weather would be cold, but this did not seem too much of a challenge. I took that in my stride and imagined just wearing my warmest clothes.

Several weeks later though, while remembering the consul's comment about the weather; I decided to take five layers of ski clothing. Surely this would be more than enough? I was working in the USA soon after the New Year, and the simplest way to fly there was across the Pacific via Korea. The subsequent flight with Korean Airlines to Ulaanbaatar was very smooth, apart from departing five hours late.

There were just a few of us on the plane arriving at Genghis Khan international airport, no less. The immigration lady in her glass booth was sleeping. I knocked on the glass, said hello through a little window but her dreams were too deep. After some minutes she woke, but did not look entirely with this world. Instead of taking down my passport information from the main page, she recorded the details from an old and expired Russian visa. I wondered if this script was easier. She was very kind in her half sleep.

My guide, Mr Batzorig Nergui from Juulchin Tours, was just outside the baggage claim. I was relieved to learn that he had been able to take advantage of my lateness to eat dinner with his family, and that traffic was now light. His car was in a parking lot just opposite the terminal.

Crossing the road, I was hit by a new sensation. The only other time I have been 'arrested by the weather' was leaving the airport in Singapore and feeling slammed into a wall of humidity. This time I felt punched in the chest by a two foot wide block of ice. My heart retreated, all my internal organs seemed to shrink at once and my chest was immediately tight. I was so glad the car was only a few more yards away and very grateful to climb inside. Even

243

though the old Mercedes heater was on, we spoke with frosty breath all the way to town. I asked the temperature and Batzorig replied, "Minus 40 degrees." I was about to ask him whether this was in Fahrenheit or Celsius before remembering this is the only temperature on which both scales agree. Batzorig mentioned casually the possibility of camel riding in the snow, but my reaction told him that this did not seem thrilling at the moment.

Everybody in the Ulaanbaatar hotel was so openhearted with the customary calmness of their Buddhist culture. I met a descendant of Genghis Khan in the bar. He seemed a perfect lookalike and insisted on making me a hat before Friday. I had a sense that this trip was going to be fabulous. My room seemed like a giant suite. I wondered if they had upgraded me because minus 40 was not exactly the peak tourist season.

I slept like a baby before rising at dawn and carefully putting on many layers of specialist clothing from earlier ski holidays. Batzorig arrived after breakfast and we set off to visit the temples.

Despite being wrapped up like an Egyptian mummy, after about two minutes outside, I felt that someone had grabbed both sides of my face and stretched the skin taut like a drum. At first this was painful, and then quite scary. As if the skin would split if I touched my cheeks. The next sensation was of sharp spikes, like icicles in the nose. Instinctively, I moved my nose constantly like a rabbit does, up and down and sideways in varying circles to stop any ice forming inside. Are rabbits from Mongolia, I wondered. Batzorig smiled and told me, "Now you know why we have small noses."

Looking at the sky, the cold had eaten all the clouds for breakfast. This might explain why Mongolia boasts the largest number of sunny days anywhere in the world. I just wished the sun could warm up more quickly. Diving into another temple allowed my face to unfreeze.

We visited the Gandantegchinlen Monastery, the 'Great Place of Complete Joy'. Inside is a giant statue of Avalokiteśvara, the embodiment of compassion and apparently the tallest indoor statue in the world at 26 metres and a half.

We spent a long time listening to their chanting prayers, aware of the benefits of

staying inside and hoping that the sun would climb a little to warm the air. But, on my way outside again, I confessed to Batzorig that I was not going to make it. Despite wearing five layers of ski gear, the wind cut straight through and made me feel naked. I asked him if we could make a detour to the market so I could find some proper Mongolian clothing.

We found an absolutely divine coat, covered head to toe with embroidered brown silk. The lining was made from baby lambskins, the cuffs were beaver, and the buttons silver. A matching hat was filled with goose down and fox fur. I had not enjoyed buying a coat so much since my first Afghan in 1972, but this Mongolian coat is regal by comparison. Not only that, but the cost was less than my ski anorak. Once I was all buttoned up, I felt like toast. Back on my tour of town, visiting museums and temples, many Mongolians looked as if imagining me an important herdsman and made admiring comments. At lunch Batzorig advised me to eat meat, meat and more meat. Apparently, this is how to release energy during the day in cold temperatures.

In the following days we passed through Terelj National Park with gorgeous scenery, many sacred mounds, and the granite rock formation of a giant turtle.

We came to a nomad camp with Gers, or Yurts, where we stopped to meet all those inside. The first lady host was so overwhelmed by my coat that she excused herself to change into the coat she wore to her wedding. Together we looked a splendid pair while she treated me to four-year-old frozen yoghurt sticks together with a ritual of salty milk drinking followed by snuff.

We wandered in the steppe looking for Przewalski's horses. These truly wild Mongolian horses were locally extinct before being reintroduced following a breeding programme in Europe. Drifting around, the snow was not deep, but like a sprinkling of icing sugar which blows continually across the ground. The grazing animals seem to be eating a little 'powdered water' together with the few blades of plants as they chew. I marvelled at how Mother Nature has provided a perfect solution to enable animals to 'drink' in a climate where everything would otherwise be inaccessible under ice.

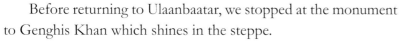

Before returning to Ulaanbaatar, we stopped at the monument to Genghis Khan which shines in the steppe.

I mused on the irony of Genghis Khan's head being 40 metres above ground while the temperature was 40 degrees under. Having climbed up some steps inside the horse's hind legs, I observed the local 'town' from a viewing platform in the horse's mane. The Yurts below looked tiny.

Whilst viewing them, the memory of the museum in Ulaanbaatar showing the vast extent of the Mongol empire came back to me. How was it possible that these nomad herdsmen, from a land of 800,000 souls, had expanded their influence to conquer a hundred million people all the way to and including the Black Sea in the thirteenth century?

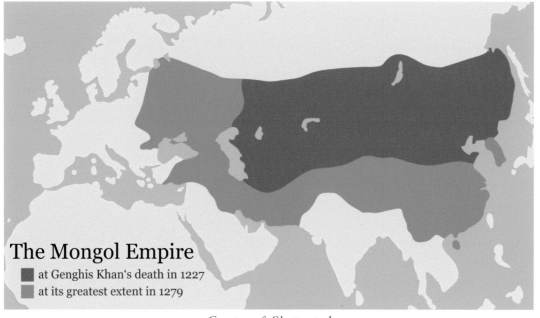

The Mongol Empire

■ at Genghis Khan's death in 1227
■ at its greatest extent in 1279

Courtesy of Shutterstock

Despite the cold, which seemed to be giving me a form of altitude sickness, there was something else which made me shudder even more – the stories of Communist purges in the 1930s that killed one in every twenty souls. Mirroring the repression of Stalin, those considered 'enemies of the revolution' were tortured and imprisoned in remote camps. Academia and Buddhism were a particular focus for execution.

In 1990 Mongolia emerged again from this tragic history and, at the time of my visit, was noted internationally as the freest and most democratic country in Asia.

The only monastery which functioned during the earlier dark chapter was Gandantegchinlen where I began my tour, and from where I emerged to find the coat. I learned that the golden statue of Avalokiteśvara and compassion was rebuilt in 1996, with over two thousand precious stones, and many local Mongolian donations. This world's tallest internal statue perfectly reflects the enormous compassion of these wonderful people.

I read a few months later that my visit had been during one of the worst winters, when almost one in five of all Mongolian animals perished in the cold. The magnificent coat had, however, much more warmth in her story.

Flying to Inner Mongolia via Beijing with two bags, the only way to carry everything was by wearing the coat. On arrival at my hotel, my attention was captured by a couple getting married. They asked me to join them in a picture because of my attire. They were so beautiful, both inside and out and I felt small next to the groom, literally and otherwise.

I tried to wear the coat in London once or twice, but the climate is so mild that I began to melt as fast as an ice-cube in a microwave. After a few English winters of being unable to wear the Mongolian 'microwave', I knew instinctively that the coat was destined for the greatest teacher in my life and a very dear friend, Martín

Prechtel. The New Mexico winters in the mountains are very cold. I have known Martín for over a quarter of a century. He is a shaman from the Tzutujil Mayan in the highlands of Guatemala. He loves Mongolia and his two youngest children are named after Mongolian nature.

I decided to surprise him.

I knew he was going to give a talk at a church in Wisconsin, so I flew to Chicago with a large bag hiding my offering. I sat in a pew about five rows from the front and he was delighted to see me. He asked why I had come, but I froze completely as if 40 degrees under and could not speak. Only after his talk was I able to go up to him and present the coat.

In return he taught me a much more priceless lesson. That I had frozen because of my fear of the deepest part of me that is compassionate. I had never imagined how the most precious part of me could be more terrifying than any of the demons. Martín was very loving, and gave me a high five that made me feel twenty six and a half metres tall.

There is no doubt that the previous paragraph sparked me to write *Mannership*.

The subtitle of *Mannership; Seeking a Source of Self-Destruction* is really about a search for beauty. The next and final chapter of this book reflects another of Martín's teachings; an awareness of ancestral lessons in our etymology. The onward journey to Hohhot highlighted a difference between China and Britain when it comes to 'winning', and this is explained in the next chapter.

As well as wandering all over the globe, I discovered that there was a much greater need to 'wander into my own mind'.

ANCESTRAL LESSONS

To help understand our different histories, there are many important messages that our ancestors want us to hear, or see. They are still speaking to us if we are willing to listen. A hearing person experiences words as sounds. Perhaps there is less need to look at words or to wonder where they come from. Our ancestors can come to life when we start to investigate words with a different listening ear, and take a fresh look. All of a sudden we can find mysterious aspects of our culture which are very much alive. Like a rock in the garden. As we move her, all kinds of insects and beetles can be seen scurrying about. They must have been there a very long time but we hadn't looked before.

Not only may secrets of our own culture be revealed, but similarities and differences with different cultures might also appear. For example, take the English word 'liver'. The word hints at living. But why is life attached to this organ which we call the 'liver'? In Chinese, a liver is written as 肝. The left hand character, in ancient times, was used for a 'person'. 肝 could therefore be anciently understood as 'person stand up'. A liver is connected in English with living and in Chinese with a 'person standing up'. Not so dissimilar after all. Perhaps the coincidence reminds us that to be a real person we must 'stand up' and live spontaneously.

Watching with the eye of a deaf person, and listening with the ear of someone whose hearing has returned, made me aware of a frequent misfit in the phrase; "I will try." Uncannily often, when someone told me they would 'try', my deaf-sight told me they were not even going to bother. Their speech and their body language seemed quite disconnected whilst uttering this specific phrase. Suddenly, I realised that the verb 'to try' has opposite meanings in English. The meaning can either be 'to attempt', or 'to frustrate', as in a child who is 'trying'. The question of why my ancestors gave this word a double meaning seemed an intriguing line of inquiry. Also, how fascinating that people unconsciously, but frequently, use this particular phrase when quite ambivalent about their likely future effort in the subject.

Was this a one off, like a lone beetle under the rock? Or was there lots of life, which had been missed, under similar rocks? The only answer was to look under more rocks, which reminded me of my childhood in the woods. The range of beetles and other insects in their colonies fascinated me.

In the English language, we have a significant number of words which contain two opposite meanings, known as 'contronyms'. That we have even a name for this family of words is relevant. We may have more contronyms than all other

European languages combined. Why would a language, which can be so precise, have so many words implying opposite meanings? The 'surprise' is even more telling when we discover that many of these words relate to subjects of the greatest significance to the British culture. Many of our contronyms include ambiguity on whether we are being helped and free on the one hand or whether we are being hindered, obstructed or made captive on the other. These are not small nuances. On the contrary, the most common subjects of our contronyms are perhaps the most important desires of British culture – individuality, independence, and freedom of expression. Immediately, this reminded me of my Viking and Victim roots and of Martín Prechtel's telling me; "…you come from a people that wrestles with that." Have our ancestors been sending a clear message, and have we been deaf?

The first family of contradictions relate to whether we are free or the opposite, whether we are helped or obstructed. Just a few examples are considered below:

Bound means 'heading for some destination', and can even imply joy and anticipation as in 'leaps and bounds'. Except that the word also means 'tied up';

Fast means either quickly or tied up, like 'made fast' as slaves often were, showing that the two opposite meanings in 'bound' were not an exception;

To **bolt** means both to secure and to flee;

A **trip** is both a journey as well as an obstacle which makes us fall;

Left can either mean departed (as if on a trip) or remained as in left behind;

To **buckle** means both to 'connect with' as well as 'to bend and give way under pressure';

To **hold up** means both 'to lift and support' as well as to 'attack for gain' as in a bank robbery;

To **fix** means either to repair or to neuter by castration or spaying.

* * * * *

Some of our contronyms are also connected with importance and hierarchy:

A **peer** is both a person of nobility and an equal colleague;

A **custom** is both a common practice for everyone as well as a specially made treatment for a few;

A **variety** can be either a specific type, or alternatively an indiscriminate number of types;

A **model** is both an exemplar as well as a copy.

* * * * *

When we speak of management or leadership the ambiguity in our language continues:

To **overlook** means both to supervise and to neglect;

Oversight can mean either to have supervision of, or forgetting to look;

To **give out** means both to provide as well as to collapse due to insufficiency;

To **flog** means to sell or promote, as well as to beat with a whip;

Finished can either mean successfully completed or ended by destruction;

To **screen** can be to exhibit as in a cinema or to hide and shield from view;

Likewise, **transparent** means both invisible and obvious at the same time;

To **sanction** means to give permission as well as to punish or boycott;

To **wind up** means either to end or to begin, as in provoke or wind up a toy.

* * * * *

An ambiguity is also found in the expression 'to fight with France' which can mean both to fight alongside France as well as to fight against France. Considering how often we changed alliances in European wars, perhaps this lack of clarity is unsurprising. Apparently, in the last thousand years, the number of wars between Britain and France is the same number as those in which we joined together to wage war on a third party. In our history, fighting with or against France is clearly much of a muchness, as the words in our language can imply.

The Latin word 'sanguine' has evolved in English, perhaps because of our Viking invaders, to mean either confidently cheerful or bloodthirsty. Most of us might say that sanguine is therefore a contronym. Erik the Red from Norway, whose murderous activities caused him to be regularly expelled westwards until he settled in Greenland around 982 CE, might have felt the two meanings of sanguine went hand in hand. Perhaps Tolui, Genghis Khan's son who butchered the great city of Merv, would share the sentiment.

The English also have a famous butcher, Dick Turpin, who 'operated' primarily in the 1730s. When he wasn't relieving animals of their skin and bones, he made a living fleecing folk on their journeys. He is perhaps our best known 'highwayman'. If English is not my reader's first language, the word highwayman does not mean someone who collects tolls on the turnpike, but the meaning is not dissimilar. We English love our double negatives; they allow more ambiguity to creep in. We prefer the term 'highwayman' because someone who indulges in 'highway robbery' is much too definite a term.

The early 18th century was a time when one could travel comfortably by horse-drawn stagecoach, if one had the means. Unfortunately, Dick Turpin and his gang descended upon such travellers with regularity. Like vultures taking easy pickings.

The records say he relieved Mr Godfrey of six guineas and a pocket book on Hounslow Heath. Relieved? Were the six guineas and the pocket book so heavy that Mr Godfrey needed relief? Dick struck again in Epping Forest, depriving a man from Southwark of his belongings. The word 'depriving' seems chosen for ambivalence, as if wishing to highlight the elegant way the skin of belongings had been masterfully removed from a lamb. Where is the rage? Or was road rage something which only came in our current generation? Dick became more audacious, with more blood involved, until he was caught and executed at York in 1739. He was romanticised in English folklore, together with his magnificent horse 'Black Bess', as if many in our culture wished they could have done the same. Actually many did, but more often overseas where the arm of the law was less of a burden.

Writing this chapter, and thinking of a few contronyms, immediately reminded me of Dick Turpin, beginning with the era of fast stagecoaches and horses with travellers bound with free spirit on an exciting trip…

until one bumps into Mr Turpin. Quite a trip. All of a sudden the passengers are 'held up'. Some were unlucky enough to be tied or bound with rope while relieved of objects of more interest to Mr Turpin.

The word 'coach', as in stagecoaches, comes from Hungary. Specifically from the village of Kocs, pronounced 'coach', where steel spring suspension was invented in the early 1400s. The more comfortable ride was much in demand across Europe and gave rise to 'coach' in most European languages. In Oxford University slang, 'coach' was first used in the 1830s to denote a tutor who carried one smoothly through the examination phase. This meaning caught on and prevails today.

One has to smile deliciously at the way our ancestors polished these words like smooth pebbles on the beach. Perhaps they chuckled as they knew all along what they were up to. There is another ancient possibility. Could contronyms have originally meant only one thing, but our desire to 'run away' from something fearful had introduced the idea of an opposite meaning? The opposite meaning may have offered some safety from the truth. Perhaps there is more safety if we pretend that confidently cheerful and bloodthirsty are polar opposites, and instead go to movies where these two are only paired on the screen.

There seem to be so many lessons from our ancestors waiting to be found once we are willing to look underneath the rocks. We might even remember that a rock is both a noun for something immobile as well as a verb for an action of doing the opposite, like rocking a baby. Rocking a baby is not entirely benign; there is a sense of something unsettling about the activity…

Ever since my silent years, the origin of words has always aroused my curiosity. The English, Dutch and Danish form a close genetic cluster. One of the traits we three nations share is sarcasm. My family name, Goodwin, is a very ancient name for 'a protector and a friend', but this name is also used for the most sly and treacherous part of the waters off the South-East coast of Britain. These shifting sands, which are constantly altered by the tides and currents, are sarcastically named the 'Goodwin sands' and have sunk over two thousand ships in the last thousand years.

The thought which occurred to me was whether my island culture found a way to dissipate fear with laughter, packaged as a silent pair. Is this why sarcasm is so important to us? Because sarcasm enables a biting and cutting remark to be sugar coated with humour? And the 'deadpan face' can preserve our stiff upper lip while serving delicious malice. Is sarcasm a very precise and directed form of irony?

This selection of some English contronyms might seem to my reader a fun interlude except that the ancestors clearly want to be heard. We really cannot ignore how many of our 'contronyms' relate to whether we have freedom or not, particularly whether we are helped or hindered. The words contain metaphors in our island psyche which are serious matters. However, realising how many previous generations shared my internal struggles and contradictions was comforting. We clearly come from a people that wrestle with these contradictions.

On my travels, an interest in etymology often made me ask the origins of a word in another culture, like the Chinese character for liver. Since I speak no Chinese, etymology in China is like doing a jigsaw puzzle in reverse. Starting with the full picture of a character, I disassemble the components until each piece of the puzzle has only a part of the original. Next, I ask, what does that part mean? Mirth and enthusiasm can follow. So far, my Chinese hosts have always seemed to enjoy the game. Let me give an example.

好赢 While in Hohhot, the capital of Inner Mongolia, my curiosity asked them how to write the name Goodwin. To which the reply was simply to draw the image shown here. Undeterred, the next question was how to disassemble the parts. First of all, my host explained that there were two characters. The one on the left, pronounced 'Hao', means 'good' and the one on the right, pronounced 'in', means 'win'.

Simple enough, except my curiosity runs much deeper. How then does the one on the left mean good? The patient answer was that "…'Hao' is also made up of the two characters for female and male, which is good," they said with a sweet smile. That seemed easy enough. Just to check, the left-most part, 女 means female. My enthusiasm for this new game encouraged my hosts to play more. The character on the right was explained as being made up of five other characters. On the top, sits the character for death. Below death is a character looking like a post box which is mouth. Then, under mouth, is a triplet of characters, meaning moon, money and normal. Naturally, I asked how one derives 'win' from a combination of 'death', 'mouth', 'moon', 'money', and 'normal'. This caught my audience off guard and led to much animated banter between them. The answer was not obvious and instead a reply at breakfast was promised.

The following morning's breakfast included a delicious reply. "Well," they said, "the character 月, which is usually translated as moon or month, used to mean a person in ancient times." They had discovered overnight that, during the time of Chairman Mao, this character changed her meaning from person to moon. They showed me many other characters relating to the body, such as waist, muscle, and of course liver, which included a moon or month. They were more surprised than me. The discovery of the meaning of liver was just a bonus along the way. Finally, having asked again how these five characters make up win, their response was amazing. "The character for death on top means that one's mind has 'overcome death', and therefore implies alertness of mind. The mouth in the middle means a good communicator. The three characters underneath suggest supporting features. Firstly, the support of people; secondly, the 'shell' refers to the support of many assets rather than just money; and thirdly, the character for 'normal' comes from one of our fairy tales of a fairy who came down to earth."

They concluded with "Altogether, 'in' means an alert mind, a good communicator with the support of the people, having both tangible and intangible assets, and down to earth."

Wow, I thought, quite a winner.

Naturally this is a joyous memory and can often be shared. Just a few days ago, meeting a Chinese couple on the train to Cambridge, led to the opportunity for me to offer this knowledge. They seemed as amazed as my hosts in Hohhot. Or were they just being polite?

By contrast, the English word 'win' comes from our genetic cousins, the Dutch and Danish. The verb has origins in 'strive', 'struggle' and 'fight', presumably successfully. Clearly, 'win' means something quite different to the ancestors of the English and the Chinese.

Other cultures have very different lessons in their etymologies. The range of paradigms is much wider than we realise 'in the West'. Perhaps the most important lesson for us is to jettison completely the idea that one way of life suits all. We have spent far too long promoting our ideas of leadership, governance, political systems and values. We need to help build a future on the premise that different paradigms are equally valuable.

In English, racism is a noun meaning, "…prejudice, discrimination, or antagonism directed against a person or culture on the basis of their ethnic group." The meaning should perhaps include a few extra words such as 'on the basis of their paradigms or beliefs'. Attacking beliefs, and calling them 'heresies', has also been particularly poisonous. In my book, *Mannership*, I discovered that different religions share much more than they differ. We need all of them to understand each other, just as we need all the plants to survive.

EPILOGUE

I regret the ending of this book as there are so many wonderful lands and stories I should have included. Some of my experiences in the Gilbert Islands are told in Mannership and the companion volume Mannership III. My journey across Africa in 1973 is told separately in Khartoum to El Aaiun.

The simple truth is that I have found warmth in every country I visited. I would have liked to tell you about all 169 of them.

Among the stories I would like to have included was my return to Sri Lanka when Booker Tate was responsible for the Pelwatte Sugar Company. Most of our challenges related to elephants with a sweet tooth. When we built a moat, the elephants pushed the earth back to make a bridge. When we put up an electric fence, bull elephants lay down and pushed the pylons over. The families then walked carefully with toes between the wires. Elephants are so nifty and smart as I learned in the Kandy Perahera. In the end, with help from the Ministry of Agriculture, several families of elephants were caught by tranquiliser darts and taken to a more northerly part of the Sri Lanka. Years later, on my most recent visit, the mahouts asked why I hadn't just left a part of the farm for the elephants to chew. But, I had to admit, we had not thought of this possibility.

When I first visited Costa Rica, I sensed something quite different which I could not quite put my finger on. My deaf-sight often 'smells' something. I subsequently learned that, in 1948, there was a civil war following the outgoing Government's annulment of the election result. After 44 days of strife, the true victor of the election was installed. The following year; the new Government abolished the National Army and decided to use the budget for health and education instead. I thought that this alone warranted a story. I take my hat off to them, and their wisdom. I think that every country in the Americas, from Mexico to Chile, has suffered a military coup – or domestic military interference in elections – since 1945, and most commonly in Argentina or Bolivia. One way to avoid military coups is by not having a military. While enjoying many visits to Costa Rica as a consultant, and enjoying excursions to her jungles, volcanoes, flora and fauna, I often thought of other countries that could have followed this lead. Instead, there have been 64 'military coups' in the Americas since the abolition of Costa Rica's army.

I could tell you of the special fish and crab tasting pork in Tonga, where pigs go fishing on the ocean reef. But, I could go on for a long time. There is so much more.

I have decided to include just one more story here, which is not really a chronicle but an account of some events spread over many years. This shows how little islands can help their former colonial masters, as in 'The Letter that got carried away'. This book began in The Gilbert Islands, Kiribati, and we could digest a concluding offering from the Central Pacific.

THE LETTER THAT GOT CARRIED AWAY

Background

On arrival in the Gilbert and Ellice Islands Colony in 1975, I was made aware of the local taxation system. An annual levy, payable by all over the age of eighteen, was appropriately called 'The Head Tax'. We would refer, in England, to such a tax as a Poll Tax, but Head Tax actually describes the system rather more precisely. I paid my dues on time; the amount was modest for a Government officer and did not occupy much of my attention.

Several months later, following my promotion to District Officer, Tarawa, the subject was still not much of a concern, even though I became responsible for tax collection to finance the town, urban and rural councils and their services. The tax had been there for as long as anybody could remember. The amount was the same for everyone. Nobody questioned this burden.

Knowing myself to be the last British District Officer before independence, I threw myself into every challenge as a matter of urgency. I said, during local meetings of elders in the village maneabas, that the time for a foreigner to decide had passed. Soon they would be independent and, in their last two years as a British Colony, they should tell me what they wanted. I would devote my energy to carry out their wishes. Initially, there was no sign of trouble. I had not seen the storm coming.

Everything which the elders suggested made perfect sense. One after another, each extra service was provided by the local

261

councils. We started with modest ideas such as the introduction of bus shelters in every village. They were simple, used only local materials, and could be produced by the villagers themselves. We cleaned the villages and captured stray dogs.

We built a botanical garden on the Island of Betio. This was planted adjacent to 'Red Beach', the location of one of the toughest battle in US Marine Corps history, in November 1943. Over three thousand marines were killed or wounded on this tiny islet of Tarawa Atoll. The garden was also next to the wharf for the inter-islet ferry, where passengers could wait in the shade of Central Pacific plant varieties.

The elders became more enthusiastic about what we could achieve. I added my suggestions for protecting the environment, which were warmly received.

In our enthusiasm, we had not noticed how quickly we were running out of funds for new ideas. There was no possibility to borrow and we had to choose between reducing the number of new projects or increasing taxation. Perhaps this should not have been a surprise. Neither was palatable.

But, on considering the matter, my mathematical mind noticed that the problem was different. We were only collecting about sixty percent of the taxes due. I pointed this out to the elders; if everybody paid, we would have enough money for everything they wanted.

The Head Tax was about twenty Australian Dollars and did not seem too much for everyone to pay. We decided this was quite unfair; those who hadn't paid should pay. At first, the elders decided to ask their villagers directly, but only a few more paid. They decided we should prosecute the non-payers. After all, maybe next year even more might decide not to pay if there were no consequences, and everything we were achieving might unravel.

The storm and the letter

Christmas was approaching, although there was little sign of upcoming festivity. The hundred and something degree heat with ninety-nine percent humidity was constant all year. Any childhood imagery of a tree or ornaments wrapped with tinsel wilted in the sun.

The elders had all agreed that we would have to enlist the help of the Island Court. Trusting the English Legal system was the answer, naturally. But this quickly embroiled me in an avalanche of unfavourable winds. The local magistrates were not keen to rule in my favour and preferred the various tactics of the defendants. This was enough to tear the hair out of a young District Officer. The idea of the Island Councils failing on my watch was not appealing. The elders, and the councillors, supported the idea of the courts and sympathised, but to no avail.

Although a few of the court cases for unpaid taxes went in my favour, my alarm was raised by something else. The cost of the court cases began to exceed the extra revenue. I hadn't thought of that. Now we were facing a quicksand. After all the court cases, we would have even less money than we started with. In my desperation, and youthfulness, the next step was simply to elevate the urgency. 'The Letter' was written to the Attorney General to ask for help. At the time, I was sure this was the only way to unblock the situation. Something had to happen.

My kind and charming assistant, Erihapeti, typed my hand-written missile carefully. There was a giant sigh of relief as I signed. The cat was now thrown among the pigeons, I thought.

Surely there was no risk from being honest for the benefit of everyone? After all, the wishes of the elders were sound and would be appreciated by all.

GILBERT AND ELLICE ISLANDS COLONY

Telegrams:

DISTRICT TARAWA

District Commissioner's Office

Tarawa

Gilbert Islands

26 January 1977

To: The Honourable the Attorney General, Bairiki

Dear Sir,

I wish to make representation in the strongest possible terms about the state of the Judiciary. In my opinion it is not about to collapse but has already collapsed.

2. Cases are taking an inordinate time to be heard and the most absurd decisions are being made by the courts. In the event of fines for criminal cases only a minute proportion are being paid and next to no action is being taken to remedy the situation. The most trivial cases are finding their way up to the High Court and the Betio Town Council alone has now 13 cases which are pending for the High Court, none of which in my opinion should have gone beyond the Island Court. Soon even the High Court may become bogged down with our trivial cases.

3. I wish however to complain about the way in which a case was conducted in the Senior Magistrate's Court on Monday in which I represented the Betio Town Council as the plaintiff. The defendant was heavily under the influence of alcohol, repeatedly swore and abused both myself and the court. I rarely completed a sentence without loud interruptions from his swearing and found it impossible to state my case. I was denied the right to ask questions of a witness because the defendant did not wish it and the Magistrate accepted his wish. I repeatedly asked the Magistrate if some form of order could be established but nothing was forthcoming and the case was concluded by the Magistrate saying that he did not understand it. It was not a difficult case, in fact I can hardly think of a simpler one.

4. A recently appointed Magistrate has made a number of infringements against the law and although both Government and the Council have tried to prosecute him it has not been possible since no other Magistrate is willing to hear the case.

5. I would be grateful if urgent consideration could be given to the state of the Judiciary and I also feel that the Magistrates need some training.

Yours faithfully

(Mark Goodwin)

District Officer Tarawa

While waiting for a response from the Attorney General, the court cases occupied much of my time. The only 'upside' of the court was that the thatched courtroom was next door to my office, on the wharf of Betio islet.

Betio was a half-hour ferry journey from my home in Bairiki village. Ten days after the letter, and having just arrived on the ferry, I discovered a senior police officer was interviewing Erihapeti. I recognised him, Batriti from Bikenibeu. That was very odd. Why hadn't he waited for me? Clearly this was not a social call. What could he be asking?

I continued to review my incoming mail – there was nothing particularly urgent. The policeman, Batriti, came to my office. Graciously asking him to be seated, we greeted each other warmly. He had a 'buff file' with the contents all kept in order by a small green cord and two metal toggles which fitted neatly through a hole in the top left hand corner of every page. My letter to the Attorney General was top of his file, I noticed.

He began by asking if this was my letter.

I wondered why he asked; surely he could explain? My limited knowledge of English Law should be sufficient to give me some clues. Quite calmly Batriti explained that I was to be prosecuted for 'Contempt of Court', an offence which could lead to imprisonment.

I was shocked. This was another calamity I had walked into. The quicksand was going to swallow me up. There I would be, in prison, while the Councils became bankrupted by the cost of the courts exceeding the revenue. I could imagine the local unrest and my fault entirely. This was a moment for thinking clearly, being courteous and kind, while attempting to figure out an 'escape' from this rather unexpected denouement. I listened carefully. Batriti explained that he had just interviewed and taken a statement from Erihapeti. She confirmed that she typed the letter on my instruction.

Quite calmly, I asked, "I see, and what do you want from me?"

"I have instructions to get a statement from you confirming that this is your letter," he replied.

There seemed little option but to comply, but the situation had clearly got out of hand. How could I rescue myself? What recourse was possible? I decided to change the tone of the conversation, to talk about all the wonderful projects of the council and my frustration that we were unable to finance them because of the non-payment of taxes. Perhaps he would have some sympathy, but he was unmoved. I was trying to buy time when I asked for 'clarification'. The urgency and gravity of the case before me was more than challenging.

I asked again. "Let me be sure that I understand. Is there anything else you need apart from this signed statement from me?"

"No, that's all," he answered.

I continued to go with the flow. "So, your task is simply to obtain from me a signed statement confirming that this is my letter." He nodded. I wanted so much for the letter to just disappear; how had I been so foolish? Suddenly a plan appeared to me. I told Batriti that he was doing his job properly and politely, for which he had my support. I felt sure we would resolve everything to make everyone happy.

After a few more questions, I summarised the situation simply. "The Attorney General has asked you to get this signed statement from me, and you will be happy if we can quickly conclude this matter with a new letter from me stating this clearly. We have agreed that this can be handwritten on your statement form, which I could then sign. That would make both of you happy."

Hoping that my plan would work, I could not have been more courteous. He seemed grateful. I started to write my statement as he requested. Just before I signed, I asked once again. "It seems that we both agree that the key to this whole matter is whether this letter is mine". He agreed. I continued, "It would only seem fair, since this letter is really mine, that I should be allowed to have my letter back." Batriti could not see any reason why not. I continued by encouraging him that we had both agreed this letter was mine after all.

He struggled with the treasury tag at the top left of his folder. I did not want to betray my anxiety that he might change his mind and tried to distract myself. I wondered where those tags all came from. Silly me, I

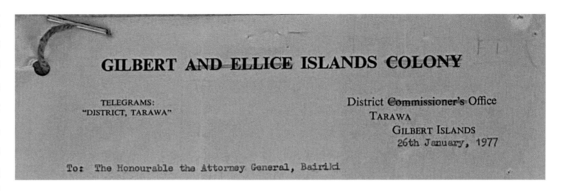

GILBERT AND ELLICE ISLANDS COLONY

TELEGRAMS:
"DISTRICT, TARAWA"

District Commissioner's Office
TARAWA
GILBERT ISLANDS
26th January, 1977

To: The Honourable the Attorney General, Bairiki

thought, they are called 'India tags'. Carefully he passed the metal toggle and green cord through the hole, and as I passed over my signed statement, he gave me back my letter.

We shook hands warmly as he left to get the ferry back to the Attorney General's Office in Bairiki. I felt a distinct sigh of relief. He was happy having achieved his mission, and the Attorney General would be happy that all was set for my trial. But, I knew there was no photocopier on the island. My relief came from a realisation that, in court, I could simply ask which letter they were referring to. What were we talking about? I hoped this would be the end of the matter.

The letter is now framed on my study wall, on my left, as this chronicle is written.

The outcome

There was no time to dwell on the potential court case and I was not going to tempt fate. Instead, I felt the time had come to completely rethink everything; to go back to the drawing board. I must use my temporary reprieve wisely.

At a meeting with the elders, I proposed we should just start again. Let us imagine we had no taxes at all and were going to start from scratch. I had never felt so energised. "Let us design a fair tax system which is easy and cheap to administer. If we taxed each house instead of each head, this would reduce the number of tax payers. Also, the houses do not move frequently and one of our difficulties is that we do not know who is living everywhere; the administration of finding everyone is hard." They all agreed, and started to catch my enthusiasm like a blazing fire when I dropped the next ideas. "We could have six categories of house. The first category would be for a house which was built entirely from local materials, with nothing imported in the structure." They listened with interest, imagining the locally built houses. "For these houses, why don't we make them exempt from tax? Often they are occupied by families who have no cash income at all. They fish and build from nature. They do not pollute the environment." The elders looked at me with astonishment. "And then we can increase the tax on those who have bigger houses, especially those who have purchased corrugated iron roofing or brick walls." I could not resist my last line. "So this means that people like me, and the Attorney General will have to pay more." They all laughed.

We voted unanimously to change the law on the spot. The solution was simple. We were able to reduce the average rate of tax by a third and exempt many who had little or no cash income. But, with a reduced cost of collection and if a greater proportion paid, we could finance all the projects and services we wanted. In the end, everybody was happy. The 'Head Tax' was buried by the threat of sending me to prison. Necessity is the mother of invention, as they say.

Next, the elders decided to move all the pigs out of the villages and to keep them in pens. Somebody took a photograph of the young District Officer making his inspection. A young engineer found we could use the sewage to generate electricity.

Before...   *...after...*   *...and the inspection.*

A postscript

Stories can have sons and grandsons. In 1987, ten years later in Britain, the Government brought in legislation for a 'Poll Tax'. I shook my head at this ridiculous idea. Now a little wiser than my letter to the Attorney General, I wrote to The Times. I was surprised when this was published, but thought nothing of the matter apart from some amusement of little islands teasing a bigger island.

Fate sometimes has a different idea.

Britain was soon in the midst of riots and fury over the 'Poll Tax'. The madness reminded me of my lessons on Tarawa.

The similarities could not be ignored;

The Council registers were inaccurate.

Those who did not pay included tenants or 'visitors' who knew they would have left before a bailiff arrived.

There was uproar among those who felt the tax was unfair as the rate was the same for rich and poor alike.

The councils were burdened with the task of pursuing large numbers of defaulters, together with court costs which reduced the final revenue.

Another poll tax

From Mr M. W. Goodwin

Sir, The urban and town councils in Tarawa, Kiribati, levied a poll tax until 1976. Of maximum revenue we managed to collect only 60 per cent, due to the difficulty of locating everybody, and incurred a collection cost of 47 per cent, an effective yield of 32 per cent. We used to prosecute for arrears, of course, even though the extra 7 per cent per annum was less than the cost of court cases.

In 1977 we abolished the poll tax and replaced it by a rate per house, dependent on size, and irrespective of location within the council area. We collected 95 per cent, with an administration cost of 15 per cent.

The extra services offered for lower taxes almost made the "rates" popular and the poll tax quickly forgotten.

Yours faithfully,
MARK GOODWIN (former District Officer, Tarawa),
14 Redcliffe Square, SW10.
May 10.

As the number of defaulters rose, and the inefficiency of collection became obvious, larger numbers of people refused to pay. According to the BBC, 30% of the UK population did not pay; the same proportion which defeated me in Tarawa.

During the Poll Tax Riots, Conservative ministers contemplated abolition of the tax but knew that Britain's Prime Minister Margaret Thatcher would not agree.

Thatcher was challenged by Michael Heseltine for the Conservative leadership in November 1990. Although she scraped through the first vote, she missed the threshold to avoid a second vote, and on 22 November 1990 she announced her resignation after more than a decade in office.

The new Prime Minister, John Major, asked Michael Heseltine to return as Environment Secretary with responsibility for replacing the poll tax.

Michael Heseltine was my local MP. He came to my office in Thame to discuss the work Booker Tate was involved with in Africa particularly. But the timing was perfect for something else. Instead, we spent most of the morning talking about the demise of the 'Head Tax' in the Gilbert and Ellice islands. Michael was fascinated by the similarities, and the solution we found with a structure of different tax bands. His eyes lit up.

Of course, we will never know, but I chuckle sometimes with the thought of how fate works her magic. Perhaps little islands had helped to solve the problem in larger islands. The British solution is an exact replica of the Tarawa one.